Proverbs for Kids

JoHannah Reardon

DEDICATION

To Jason, Anna, and Lindsey who inspired this effort. You took the Book of
Proverbs to heart and live it out daily.

NOTE TO PARENTS: WHAT IS A PROVERB?

Much of what our children see on television, at school, on the Internet, and elsewhere shows us how much we need the Book of Proverbs. All we have to do is watch people around us to figure out how to do what is wrong. It is much harder to find those who will tell us what's right. King Solomon does just that in Proverbs. It's amazing to see that people really haven't changed much in 3,000 years. Kids wanted answers then, and they still do now.

Proverbs 1:3 tells us that the Book of Proverbs will teach us how to be wise, self-controlled, honest, fair, and right. If we can help our children get a start on all those things while they are still young, think what terrific people they will be as adults!

This devotional is designed to be a platform for you to talk about the issues that your 8 to 12-year-old child faces every day. They are designed to be short and simple so that you are more likely to read them as a family consistently. What a privilege to introduce your child to the wealth in God's Word.

Before you begin, explain to your child that a proverb is a general principle that we can learn from, not a promise. For example, Proverbs 10:4 says, "A lazy person will end up poor. But a hard worker will become rich." That doesn't mean that God promises that everyone who works hard will be rich, but it's a general principle that hard workers will generally be better off financially than lazy people.

These devotions consist of parables. That means that the names and situations are fictional in order to make a point. Any similarity to real persons and situations are coincidental.

All Bible references are from the International Children's Bible® (ICB), Thomas Nelson Publishers.

DAY 1

Proverbs 1:7 "Knowledge begins with respect for the Lord. But foolish people hate wisdom and self-control."

WHO IS GOD?

During lunch at school, Chris heard a friend of his say, "God, why can't they fix a decent meal here?" Chris immediately responded by saying, "Are you asking God a question or blaming Him for the lunch? After all, He made the food just great before they cooked it here." His friend looked at him in surprise. It had been a long time since he had thought of God, even though he used His name all the time to make a point.

Proverbs 1:7 says, "Knowledge begins with respect for the Lord..." God is not an "it" or an exclamation point to our sentences. He is the all-powerful One who made the universe. He also made us with all our intricate parts and created us with a special purpose in mind. He deserves all our love, all our respect, and all our devotion. As we get to know Him, we get to know more about all of life.

—What was wrong with the way Chris' friend treated God?

—What does God have to do with knowledge?

—Why does He deserve our respect?

Further Reading: Job 28:23–28

DAY 2

Proverbs 1:8 "My child, listen to your father's teaching. And do not forget your mother's advice."

WHAT GOOD ARE PARENTS?

As Dad headed out the door to work, he called to Janet, "Don't take Maple Street on your way to the bus stop today, OK?"

Janet shrugged her shoulders. If she didn't take Maple Street, she would have to walk two extra blocks. What was the big deal? She decided to take Maple Street anyway. Halfway there she found the street and sidewalk completely torn up, workmen drilling everywhere. She had to backtrack, adding four more blocks to her walk, barely making it to the bus stop before the bus left.

Proverbs 1:8 says, "My child, listen to your father's teaching. And do not forget your mother's advice." As unreasonable as it seems at times, God has given us parents to lead us through life. If we don't listen to them, we're going to find ourselves backtracking a lot in the things that we do. Missing a bus is inconvenient, but there will be much harder things we will have to face if we don't listen to Dad and Mom. Give them a chance; they are probably smarter than you think.

—Why is it so hard to obey our parents?

—Is there anything Mom or Dad could do to make it easier?

Further Reading: Proverbs 1:9

DAY 3

Proverbs 1:10 "My child, sinners will try to lead you into sin. But do not follow them."

WHO DO YOU LISTEN TO?

"Come on, Randy. We're going to Old Man Murphy's yard for a game of football."

"Are you crazy, Joe? He's threatened to call the police if we play in his yard again."

"He's not home. What he doesn't know won't hurt him. Besides, there's no yard around big enough for a game unless we go there."

"Count me out, Joe. Seems to me Mr. Murphy has made it real clear he doesn't want us there whether he's home or not."

"Aw, you're just a chicken!"

"Let's see how brave you are, Joe, if you get caught!"

Have you ever been in a situation like that? It's really hard to go against a whole group, especially if they are doing something that looks harmless at first. God gives us a strong warning in Proverbs 1:10 against following sinners into sin. If we choose not to listen to Him, we'll have to pay for it somewhere along the line.

—Who was right, Randy or Joe?

—How can we avoid following others into sin?

Further Reading: Proverbs 1:10-12

DAY 4

Proverbs 1:19 "...Greed takes away the life of the greedy person."

THE PRICE OF BEING GREEDY

Jennifer found herself watching Maria again. Maria seemed to have everything. She was pretty, popular, and brought something new to school every day. Today she had a new watch. It had a glow-in-the-dark face and three special alarms.

As they were getting ready for gym class, Maria slipped the watch off and stuck it in her locker. Jennifer decided this was her chance. She dawdled until everyone was out of the room then quickly tucked the watch into her purse. "Maria's rich," she thought, "she can buy another one."

When gym was over, Maria discovered the loss and told the teacher. As the teacher asked the class about it, Jennifer felt a sick feeling in her stomach. Even though she got away without being caught, having the watch made her feel bad every time she looked at it. She couldn't wear it to school for fear of being caught, and she had to lie to her mother about where she got it. Jennifer began to think it had been a pretty dumb thing to do.

—Why did Jennifer take the watch?

—How did it make her feel?

—Was it worth it to her?

—What should she have done to make it right?

Further Reading: Proverbs 1:13–19

DAY 5

Proverbs 1:20 "Wisdom is like a good woman who shouts in the street."

WHAT IS WISDOM?

There was a woman whose daughter was killed by a man who was driving drunk. Of course, this woman was heartbroken, but she also wanted to do something. She wanted everyone to hear what happened to her daughter so that our country would make stricter laws. She knew that by speaking out she could help save the lives of other children.

Proverbs 1:20 says, "Wisdom is like a good woman who shouts in the street." This woman we just mentioned helps us see what wisdom is like. Wisdom is not just knowing a lot; it is a warning about life. As we gain wisdom, we are able to make good decisions that will bring us life instead of death. So how do we get wisdom? That's what the whole book of Proverbs is about. As we listen to God and His Word, we learn how to live. As Jesus lives in us, He helps us make wise choices. If you don't know Jesus as your savior, trust Him today to forgive you and guide you through the days ahead.

—How is what the woman did in our story like wisdom?

—How do we get wisdom?

Further Reading: Proverbs 1:20–22

DAY 6

Proverbs 1:23 "Listen when I correct you."

LISTEN

John always loved a dare. He had good parents who sent him to a Christian school. He had plenty of opportunity to hear what is right. But that night he was lonely. It was raining outside and there wasn't much to do. He had recently earned his driver's license so he asked for the car to go see a friend. However, instead of staying at this friend's house as his parents expected him to do, he and his friend broke into a restaurant that was closed for the evening. His friend had dared him to steal some liquor. What John didn't know was that the restaurant had an alarm that rang directly to the police station. When he was arrested a few minutes later, he felt great sorrow that he had not listened to all those who had tried to warn him.

"Listen when I correct you," God warns us. We need to let others instruct us so that we won't have to pay the terrible consequences that John paid in our story.

—What should we do if we feel like doing something we know is wrong?

Further Reading: Proverbs 1:23–25; 29–33

DAY 7

Proverbs 2:3–4 "Cry out for wisdom. Beg for understanding. Search for it as you would for sllver. Hunt for it like hidden treasure."

BETTER THAN TREASURE

Rachel was invited to a party that included a treasure hunt. Everyone at the party was divided into teams and each team was given a list of items that were hidden in the yard. Some of the items were difficult to find, such as a four-leaf clover. Many of the kids grew impatient looking through all the clover, trying to find the one with four leaves. However, Rachel knew that the first team to find all the items on the list would receive a gift certificate at the ice cream shop. This knowledge kept her looking long after everyone else wanted to quit. Rachel's team won because she refused to give up.

Our verse today encourages us to hunt for wisdom like a hidden treasure. It is easy to work hard for something immediately pleasing like ice cream. It is much more difficult to work hard for something we can't see like wisdom, but it will do us a great deal more good than the ice cream. And where do we get wisdom? From God's Word. He is the One who made us; He alone knows what is best for us. Search for Him as for a hidden treasure today.

—What made Rachel different than her teammates?

—How is God's Word like a treasure hunt?

Further Reading: Proverbs 2:1–6

DAY 8

Proverbs 2:8 "He guards those who are fair to others."

LEARNING TO BE FAIR

Brad was excited because this was his first overnight camping trip with the boy's club he had joined. He had a good friendship with most of the other guys so the idea of going camping with them sounded even more fun.

When they arrived at the campsite, they began to discuss who would stay in whose tent. No one wanted the new boy, Sam, to be in their tent. He was small and had trouble speaking without a stutter. Everyone began to make fun of him. Everyone except Brad. He remembered what it was like to be new and to have few friends. Brad was afraid to say anything at first but after a few minutes he couldn't stand it anymore. He put his arm around Sam and declared loudly that he wanted him in his tent. The other boys looked at Brad in surprise, but slowly over the weekend began to see that Sam was really a great guy and their admiration for Brad grew. After all, who wouldn't want a friend like Brad?

—How was Brad fair to others?

—How did God guard him?

—Can you think of someone you need to be fair to today?

Further Reading: Proverbs 2:7–10

DAY 9

Proverbs 2:11–12 "Good sense will protect you... It will save you from people whose words are bad."

WHERE DOES GOOD SENSE COME FROM?

"Jenny, can you come over to my house after school? A bunch of us are going to have a party. My parents don't get home from work until late so we will have lots of fun doing whatever we want!"

Jenny looked at Josie longingly. She sure would rather go to her house than to her own where she had to do her paper route. Something inside her almost said "yes", but her good sense won out. She knew it was wrong to deceive Josie's parents as well as to ignore her own duties. It was still hard, though, knowing all her friends were having so much fun.

The next day at school, she asked Josie how the party went. Josie's face fell. "The neighbor lady told my mom. I've been grounded for two weeks." Jenny thanked God under her breath that He had helped her avoid trouble once again.

God's Word gives us good sense. It helps us figure out right from wrong, and protects us from stupid decisions.

—What gave Jenny the courage to say no to Josie?

—Where do we get "good sense"?

—Take time right now to ask God to teach you "good sense" so that you will be able to make the right decisions.

Further Reading: Proverbs 2:11–15

DAY 10

Proverbs 2:20 "...wisdom will help you be a good person."

A KNOW-IT-ALL OR WISE?

Jack was a very intelligent boy. He got good grades without having to study very hard. The teacher always called on him to answer questions because she knew Jack would know. He was fantastic at trivia games, often beating the adults who were playing against him.

But Jack had one failing. He couldn't get along with other people. He tended to pick fights with the other boys, he tormented the girls to tears, and he had the bad habit of making up lies about other people.

Would you call Jack wise? Although he knew a lot of information, it did not help the way he acted. Wisdom and good actions go hand in hand.

How could Jack become wise? Only by knowing the One who is all-wise. Only Jesus Christ always did the good thing, so only through Jesus living in us can we become wise. The next time you do something wrong, ask Jesus to forgive you and to give you the strength to do the right thing the next time. That is the only way to become wise.

—How was Jack smart but not wise?

—What will show in your life if you are wise?

—Where can we get wisdom?

Further Reading: Proverbs 2:20–22

DAY 11

Proverbs 3:1–2 "My child, do not forget my teaching. Keep my commands in mind. Then you will live a long time. And your life will be successful."

HOW TO BE SUCCESSFUL

I knew a man who was a fantastic businessman. Since he was a boy, he could turn one dollar into two by making something he could sell. As he grew into an adult, he met a lovely woman, whom he married. After several years, God gave them a family — two children who were beautiful and talented.

However, this man found more enjoyment in making money than in being with his family, attending church, or getting to know God. Because he spent so much time at his business, he became tremendously rich. He could buy anything he wanted. But one day when he came home from work, there was a note from his wife. She and the children had left him because they no longer knew him. He told a friend he would give all his money away if that would help get them back. Upon hearing this, his wife said she would come back if he did just that. He did, so they are now rebuilding their lives with Jesus Christ at the center instead of money.

Success doesn't come from riches but from keeping God's commands. That is the only way anyone can find happiness.

—How did the man in the story see success?

—What was wrong with the way he looked at life?

—From where does true success come?

Further Reading: Deuteronomy 30:15–20

DAY 12

Proverbs 3:3 "Let kindness and truth show in all you do."

A TRUE FRIEND

Have you ever known anyone who seems to always be kind? Susan is such a person. She is always the first to help someone in need. If a neighbor is sick, they know Susan will be by to see them. If a person is in trouble, Susan will comfort them.

She is also truthful. If she knows that a friend has brought trouble on themselves by their sin, she gently reminds them of their need to confess their sin and experience God's wonderful forgiveness.

In a sense, Susan is the same kind of friend Jesus is —accepting and loving but firm and unwavering. People know they can count on a friend like that.

Our verse tells us today that we need to be not only kind and truthful in our hearts, but that we should let it show in all that we do. Otherwise it can't do the good for others it should. Show someone kindness and truth today and you will be on your way to making some lasting friendships.

—What two qualities should show in all we do?

—How do we become kind and truthful?

—Think of one person to go out of your way to be kind and truthful to today.

Further Reading: Proverbs 3:3–4

DAY 13

Proverbs 3:5 "Trust the Lord with all your heart. Don't depend on your own understanding."

TRUSTING

We all watched with interest as the illusionist on stage brought out a guillotine, a perfect replica of the kind used to chop off people's heads. As he explained the gruesome object, he claimed our attention when he asked for a volunteer to come put their head in it and try it out. After many moments of silence, a boy ran up to the stage and offered his neck.

Of course, the boy knew what we all knew. The illusionist was playing a trick on us. He certainly was not going to chop off anyone's head. Sure enough, after building up lots of tension, the blade came down causing the boy absolutely no harm. We all applauded with relief.

You see, the boy trusted the illusionist. He couldn't understand how the trick was going to work, but he knew the illusionist did. That's how we are to trust God with our lives. We may not know the outcome, but we know God has our good in mind. We don't depend on our own understanding but on His perfect knowledge.

—Why did the boy trust the illusionist?

—How was his trust similar to what our trust in God should be?

—Why should we not just depend on our own understanding?

Further Reading: Psalm 37:3–6

DAY 14

Proverbs 3:6 "Remember the Lord in everything you do. And he will give you success."

DON'T FORGET GOD

Rob had to give a report on the Potawatomi Indians for his English class. Having worked hard on collecting the information he needed, he felt that the material would be interesting to the others in his class. The only trouble was he had to read the report aloud in front of the class.

Rob is a good reader but a rather shy person. To stand in front of the class seemed to him the hardest thing he ever had to do. He worried about it so much that he felt sick to his stomach the night before giving the report.

His mother recognized the problem, and asked Rob if he had prayed about his feelings. She showed him Proverbs 3:6: "Remember the Lord in everything you do. And he will give you success," reminding him to trust God for the courage he needed. They prayed together that night and the churning in his stomach went away.

He prayed again as he stepped up front to read, picturing Jesus next to him. Although he felt frightened before he read, once the words started coming out of his mouth, he felt calm. Next time would be easier.

—Why was Rob so worried?

—What helped him get over his fears?

—What can you trust Jesus for today?

Further Reading: Matthew 6:33

DAY 15

Proverbs 3:7 "Respect the Lord and refuse to do wrong."

STAND BOLDLY

Tom listened with sadness as his teacher convinced the class that if they were to accept modern science, they must believe that man has evolved from lower life forms.

Tom had read several books that declared just the opposite. He knew that many modern scientists have rejected the evolutionary theory of man as improbable. Upon examining the evidence, Tom found it took much more faith to believe that man had evolved from an ameba than that God had created him. He wanted to tell the teacher all this, but fear kept him quiet.

Yet, after listening to his teacher for a few days, he just couldn't stand it anymore. He felt that if he didn't say anything that he would burst. So he boldly raised his hand, and calmly told the teacher about the research he had done. The teacher refused to rationally consider what Tom was saying, but the other students did. Several began to agree with Tom and add information of their own.

"Respect the Lord and refuse to do wrong" declares Proverbs 3:7. Tom's respect for God caused him to speak out.

—How did Tom "respect the Lord and refuse to do wrong"?

—What gave him the courage to speak up?

Further Reading: John 14:18–21

DAY 16

Proverbs 3:9 "Honor the Lord by giving him part of your wealth."

WHOSE RICHES ARE THEY?

For years our family "adopted" a boy and a girl from a different country. Even though we never met these children, we sent them money each month so they could go to school and be taught about Jesus. Their families were too poor to send them to school or even clothe them properly.

Doing this made our family see how rich we were. We all had nice clothes, attended school, and had more toys than we could play with. Sending money to children who didn't have these things became a way for us to thank God for all He had given us.

Our children couldn't afford the twenty dollars a month we sent to each of our adopted children, but they could afford extra gifts. They used their own money one Christmas to send a present. Another time they shared stickers and balloons that were their own when we wrote to their "adopted" brothers and sisters.

Maybe your church has a special offering to which you can give, or you may have a neighbor in need. Ask Mom or Dad for ways you can "honor the Lord by giving him part of your wealth".

—How does giving our money away honor the Lord?

—Decide today on a way to give some of your money to God's work.

Further Reading: I Chronicles 29:12–14

DAY 17

Proverbs 3:12 "The Lord corrects those he loves, just as a father corrects the child that he likes."

THE BEST FATHER

There once were two fathers of two different families. One father always let his children do whatever they wanted. If the child only wanted to eat desserts all day, he could. If he wanted to swim in the river in December, he could do that, too. Although his child was only twelve years old, he could take the car whenever he wanted.

The other father greatly restricted what his children could do. His child could only have dessert after eating all his dinner, including vegetables. His child not only wasn't allowed to swim in the river in December, but he had to wear a jacket and a hat whenever he went outside. Finally, although this father taught his son a lot about the family car, he knew he would not be allowed to have it until after he received his driver's license.

"The Lord corrects those he loves, just as a father corrects the child he likes." We can expect restrictions from God, too. He gives us rules to live by so that we won't ruin our lives, and he will remind us if we don't live by those rules. Don't make him teach you the hard way; listen the first time.

—Which of these fathers really loved his children?

—Why do we need to be corrected?

Further Reading: Proverbs 11–12

DAY 18

Proverbs 3:21 "My child, hold on to wisdom and reason. Don't let them out of your sight."

THE VALUE OF WISDOM

In the story *ALICE THROUGH THE LOOKING GLASS*, Alice enters a world without reason. Everything is topsy-turvy, confusing, and most of all, frustrating. No one will listen to reason or acts with wisdom. When Alice leaves the "looking glass" world, it is with relief to be back in a reasonable land again.

Sometimes our modern world is like that. Movies we watch, books we read, and people we know often act without wisdom or reason. That may seem like a lot of fun until we are in the middle of such confusion. Then, like Alice, we find that holding on to wisdom and reason is really the only way we will find a happiness that will last.

After all, God made the world using his wisdom. As we get to know God, we become wiser. Life makes sense if we live it as he intended.

—Why was Alice so frustrated in the "looking glass" world?

—How is our world sometimes like that?

—How can we hold on to wisdom and reason?

Further Reading: Proverbs 3:13–26

DAY 19

Proverbs 3:27 "Whenever you are able, do good to people who need help."

BE HELPFUL

A few months ago an elderly man in our church had a heart attack. He lives alone and has no family in the area to care for him. Our church has tried to help him by bringing him meals, magazines, and cheerful visits. He especially enjoyed seeing the children of the church. Many of them brought drawings they had done for him, or photographs of themselves.

One day I was bringing him some groceries. As I was trying to balance all the packages in my arms, I puzzled at how I was going to get the door open. Just then, James, one of the junior high age boys from our church, came by. Even though he had other plans, he stopped what he was doing to help me out and visit with this man.

James practiced Proverbs 3:27, "Whenever you are able, do good to people who need help." Look for ways to do good today whatever your plans may be.

—How did the children help the elderly man?

—What did James sacrifice to help?

—Keep your eyes open today for ways to help someone else.

Further Reading: Proverbs 3:27–30

DAY 20

Proverbs 3:31 "Don't be jealous of men who use violence. And don't choose to be like them.

AVOID VIOLENCE

In the movie we were watching, a fellow was visiting another country with some of his buddies. After a day of shopping, this fellow decided that a shopkeeper had overcharged him for one of the souvenirs he had purchased. Outraged, he and his buddies went back to the store demanding his money back. The shopkeeper refused, so the men began destroying his store. In desperation, the shopkeeper returned the man's money.

As his buddies walked out of the store, this fellow suddenly realized that this wasn't the store where he had purchased the souvenir. It actually had been the store next door.

This scene was supposed to be funny, but it wasn't. It was unjust and harmful. "Don't be jealous of men who use violence. And don't choose to be like them," declares God through this proverb. A movie can make irresponsible behavior seem acceptable just as a group of friends can do. Don't get caught in such a trap. Remember God's warning.

—How can a group make violence seem all right to us?

—How do we avoid getting caught in a group like this?

Further Reading: Proverbs 3:31–35

DAY 21

Proverbs 4:3–4 "I was once a young boy in my father's house... And my father taught me and said, 'Hold on to my words with all your heart'."

DAD HAD TO LEARN TOO

"You don't understand!" yelled Jill. "Everything is always so easy for you!" Jill had to give a piano recital this weekend and was feeling like she just couldn't do it. Her father ordered her to sit down and stick with it, which prompted her outburst. "You play so well, you wouldn't know how I feel," Jill continued.

Solomon reminded his children that he was once a young boy and had to listen to his father's advice. Jill's father grew to be a good pianist because he listened to his parents as a child. It's good for youth to remember that their parents were once in the same position that they are in now. Ask Mom or Dad to share with you one thing that they learned from their parents when they were your age.

—Why was Jill upset?

—What had she forgotten when she declared that her father didn't know how she felt?

—Name one thing your parents have taught you that you feel you should "hold on to with all your heart".

Further Reading: Proverbs 4:1–7

DAY 22

Proverbs 4:8–9 "Believe in the value of wisdom and it will make you great... Like flowers in your hair, it will beautify your life. Like a crown, it will make you look beautiful."

TRUE BEAUTY

Two new girls arrived at school on the same day. One was dressed in the latest fashion and caught everyone's attention because she was a naturally beautiful girl. The other was neat and clean, but rather plain looking in her appearance.

Because the first girl was so flashy, she got all of the attention at first, but after a while what was inside each of the girls began to come out. The first girl was selfish, gossiped about her friends, and belittled everyone around her. The second girl was a loyal friend, honest at all times, and kind even to those whom others didn't accept.

"Believe in the value of wisdom and it will make you great... Like flowers in your hair, it will beautify your life. Like a crown, it will make you look beautiful." In the long run, you will be beautiful to those who know you, not by how you look on the outside, but by who you are on the inside.

—Which of these girls would you rather have as a friend?

—How does a girl become more beautiful as she becomes wiser?

Further Reading: I Peter 3:3–4

DAY 23

Proverbs 4:14–15 "Don't follow the ways of the wicked... stay away from them and keep on going.

CHOOSE YOUR COMPANY CAREFULLY

It has always been hard for Jeremy to make friends. He is a quiet boy who tends to do things by himself. When he entered junior high school, he found a group of boys who welcomed him into their circle of friends. It was the first time any group had paid attention to him. The problem was that this group seemed to be in trouble all the time. At first the trouble was small — a visit to the principal's office, occasionally smoking a cigarette in the boy's room, and graffiti on the school grounds.

However the boys eventually began doing worse things, finally becoming drug users and thieves as they reached high school age. When several of the boys were arrested one evening, Jeremy finally came to his senses and left the group.

"Don't follow the ways of the wicked... stay away from them and keep on going." This was good advice in Solomon's day and still is now.

—What should Jeremy have done in the first place to avoid this crowd?

—What should have warned Jeremy in the beginning that this wasn't a good group to be with?

—How can you be sure you are choosing the right friends?

Further Reading: Proverbs 4:13–17

DAY 24

Proverbs 4:18 "The way of the good person is like the light of dawn. It grows brighter and brighter until it is full daylight."

OUR LIFE SHOULD BE LIKE THE DAWN

Have you ever watched the sun rise in the morning? At first the horizon begins to glow. If you look to the west, it will still be dark as night but in the east, corals begin to creep along the edge of the sky. At first these corals are a deep, dark color, but as the sun pushes upward, the whole sky begins to lighten. Gradually the shadowy colors are taken over by the sun. If it is a clear day, the sun will turn the night into such a dazzling brightness that you won't even be able to look at it.

This is how our verse describes the way of a good person. We live in a dark world because of people's sin. We are all born slaves to sin, but Jesus frees us from the hold sin has on us. We are able to light the world around us because of the work he has done in us. Let your light shine as full daylight in all you do.

—How is a good person's life like the dawn?

—What difference does that make in our world today?

Further Reading: Matthew 5:14–16

DAY 25

Proverbs 4:19 "But the wicked are like those who stumble in the dark. They can't even see what has hurt them."

WHO LIKES A BLACKOUT?

Not long ago, we had a powerful thunderstorm that knocked out the electricity of all the homes and businesses in a large radius around us. I remember groping in the dark for a candle or a flashlight. During my search I banged my shin on something. It wasn't until I found a flashlight that I discovered that my leg had struck a chair that had been pulled out of its usual position.

According to our proverb, this is the way the wicked live their lives. They don't listen to God and His Word so they stumble through life in confusion, never sure what is right or wrong. Most of the time, they don't even see the sin which is entangling them.

What a contrast to the proverb before this one! Why would anyone choose to stumble in the dark when one can walk freely in the daylight? How wonderful to know the One who makes all things bright.

—How do the wicked live?

—Is there any way out for those who stumble in the dark?

—Where does our light come from?

Further Reading: John 10:10

DAY 26

Proverb 4:22 "These words are the secret to life for those who find them. They bring health to the whole body."

WHAT LIFE IS ALL ABOUT

"I wish Jackie would come to church with me," Karen sighed. "She needs to know Jesus."

"What are you talking about?" asked Bob. "Jackie's a nice girl. She doesn't need God."

Far too many people think as Bob does. It is sometimes hard to look at a person who is basically good and see that they need Christ as their savior. But they do. The Bible tells us that "All people have sinned and are not good enough for God's glory." (Romans 3:23) Even the most pleasant person is dead in his or her sin if they don't have Jesus' forgiveness.

Jesus said, "I am the way. And I am the truth and the life. The only way to the Father is through me." (John 14:6) He has made it very clear that no matter how good we are, it will never be good enough to get to God. Jesus was the only man who has ever lived a perfect life; therefore, only through Jesus can we know God. Karen was right; Jackie does need to know Jesus. So do we all.

—What was wrong with Bob's thinking?

—Why does Jackie need Jesus even if she is a nice person?

—Who was the only one to ever live a perfect life?

Further Reading: 1 John 5:11–12

DAY 27

Proverbs 4:23 "Be very careful about what you think. Your thoughts run your life."

THOUGHTLIFE

Suzanne and Francis were two very different girls. Suzanne was always looking for a way to cheer people up. She loved to draw pictures for people, send them encouraging notes, and tell them as often as she could how much she liked them.

Francis, on the other hand, would drag those around her down. If anyone said a cheerful word to her, she was quick to answer with a sharp tone of voice. She never thought she could do anything right so she rarely tried new things or made new friends. Francis lived a lonely life.

What's the difference between these two girls? It started with their thoughts. Suzanne thought she had a lot to offer people, so she did. Francis thought she had nothing to offer, so she drove everyone away.

Proverbs 4:23 declares, "Be very careful about what you think. Your thoughts run your life." We can control our thoughts. We can fill our minds with God's word so that our lives will overflow with good things. The more we learn from Him, the better our thoughts will be, and the happier we will be. Let the thoughts that run your life be good ones.

—How were Suzanne and Francis different from each other?

—What caused this difference?

—How can we control our thoughts?

Further Reading: Philippians 4:8

DAY 28

Proverbs 4:24 "Don't use your mouth to tell lies. Don't ever say things that are not true."

TRUTH

Josh saw the fountain pen at his neighbor's house. Mr. Allen always used it to write important letters at his big oak desk. One day, as Mr. Allen left the room, Josh felt a great desire to have that pen. A moment later, it was in his pocket. Before he left the house, Mr. Allen came back to his desk and noticed it was missing. When he asked Josh about it, Josh said he didn't know what happened to it. However, as he started to leave the room, he realized his shoe was untied. As he bent over to tie it, the pen fell out of his pocket. Josh saw the hurt flash over Mr. Allen's face as he picked it up.

"Are you going to tell my mom?" Josh asked right away.

"No," answered Mr. Allen.

"You're not going to punish me at all?" asked Josh.

"Oh, you'll be punished, Josh, every time people don't believe you because you can't be trusted."

Josh left Mr. Allen's house feeling heavy and sad in his heart. He wanted to be trusted. He asked God to help him never to lie again. Today Josh is grown and is one of the most honest men around.

"Don't use your mouth to tell lies. Don't ever say things that are not true." If you follow this advice, everyone will trust you.

—What was so bad about what Josh did?

—Why don't you trust people who lie?

—Ask God to help you to be an honest person.

Further Reading: I John 2:3–6

DAY 29

Proverbs 4:27 "Do not do anything unless it is right. Stay away from evil."

GOOD CHOICES

Beth loved company. Anytime one or more persons got together, Beth was sure to be there. When she left for school that morning, her mother told her clearly that as soon as school was over to come home immediately.

When school let out, Beth remembered her mother's words and started for home. She always walked with Marsha, who lived just a few blocks from the school. As they reached Marsha's house, she invited Beth to come see how they had redecorated her room. Beth thought about her mother's orders but just couldn't wait to see Marsha's room. After all, she would just be a minute. Well, one thing led to another so that she ended up staying at Marsha's for a whole hour. She finally trudged the last couple blocks home. As she entered the front door, there sat her mother looking sad and discouraged. As it turned out, her grandmother, who lived over a hundred miles away, had stopped by for a brief visit on her way to her cousin's home. Beth had missed her and of all the company she enjoyed, Grandma was best. "Do not do anything unless it is right," our proverb warns. Beth found out why.

—Why did Beth disobey her mother?

—How would remembering Proverbs 4:27 help Beth to make the right choices?

Further Reading: Colossians 3:17

DAY 30

Proverbs 5:2 "Be careful to use good sense. Watch what you say."

WATCH WHAT YOU SAY

Ted wanted the biggest and best of everything. If someone had a bike, his was fancier. His computer had more programs than the next person's did. Even his lunches were better than everyone else's.

The trouble was that Ted let everyone know how great everything was that he owned. One day, as several kids were discussing where to have a going-away party for one of their friends, Ted volunteered his house. Another boy offered his home, but Ted insisted that his place was a lot bigger. He also was sure that his parents wouldn't mind, which he broadcast loudly to everyone.

When Ted told his parents about the party, they informed him that they would be out of town that night so the party would have to be somewhere else. Ted didn't want to admit this to all his friends so he decided to go ahead with the party anyway.

What he didn't count on was his parents talking to Randy's parents, who happened to mention the party to them. Ted's parents were furious and banned him from attending any parties for the rest of the year. "Watch what you say." It could get you in big trouble.

—How could Ted have been more careful about what he said?

—What should he have done when he found out his parents would be out of town?

Further Reading: James 3:5–6

DAY 31

Proverbs 5:3–4 "The words of another man's wife may seem sweet as honey... But in the end she will bring you sorrow. She will cause you pain like a two-edged sword."

ONE AND ONLY

Mr. Bailey had been married ten years now. His wife was a nice enough person, but after ten years she had become busy with her job and a lot of other interests. She had little time left over for Mr. Bailey.

Every day at work he saw Mrs. Carlisle. She was a little younger than Mrs. Bailey and always went out of her way to compliment him. She often brought home-baked goodies to him and had a way of smiling that made him feel good all over.

After many talks with Mrs. Carlisle, Mr. Bailey began to invite her out to lunch. Then he would make excuses to his wife about working late when he was actually with Mrs. Carlisle. Finally one day, he and Mrs. Carlisle agreed to both get a divorce so that they could marry each other. Mrs. Bailey and her two daughters were devastated but had no choice but to agree to the divorce.

Mr. Carlisle, however, asked that his wife go to marriage counseling with him so that they could improve their marriage and stay together. This is what Mrs. Carlisle had wanted all along. Mr. Bailey was left without wife or girlfriend and ended up a sad and lonely man.

—Read Proverbs 5:3-4 again. How would knowing these words have helped Mr. Bailey?

—What should he have done to help his marriage to Mrs. Bailey?

Further Reading: Proverbs 5:15–19

DAY 32

Proverbs 5:21 "The Lord sees everything you do. He watches where you go."

NO PLACE TO HIDE

Long ago God gave a man a job to do which seemed hard to the man. He was to go to a town that was an enemy of his country and tell the people there about God.

Instead of obeying God, this man went the other way, running from God. But, of course, God knew all about this. He caused a storm to threaten this man's life. Finally, after going through many difficulties, the man obeyed God and preached to the enemy city. The people there listened and turned to God.

You may recognize this as being Jonah's story. Jonah thought he could run from God but found, as our proverb states, that, "The Lord sees everything you do. He watches where you go."

It helps us to remember this when we face a decision about whether to do right or wrong. If we picture God watching us, it makes the decision to do the right thing much easier.

—What was wrong with Jonah's thinking at first?

—What are some ways you have run from God? (It may be helpful for Mom or Dad to share something first.)

—How would remembering our proverb have helped you not to run from God?

Further Reading: The book of Jonah (Read dramatically in a children's version. Let one of your children take the part of Jonah.)

32

DAY 33

Proverbs 5:22 "An evil man will be caught in his evil ways. He will be tied up by his sins as if they were ropes."

TIED UP IN SIN

Michael was a nice boy. As he grew up, he was liked by most kids his age. He liked to please everybody, so was always quick to agree with whatever they suggested.

This would have been a good quality if Michael had learned how to say "no" to evil, but when he reached his teens, his group of friends began to plan parties in a nearby woods where they would bring beer and girls. These parties became more daring the older the boys grew. Michael would feel some guilt but he quickly ignored the feeling so that his buddies would accept him.

By the time he was 18, these parties would take place two or three times a week. He never missed a one. In fact, he found he needed to drink alcohol to get going whenever he was with his friends. It seemed that he couldn't even have fun anymore without it.

As a result of this, his grades fell until he was barely passing any of his classes. Before graduating from high school, he admitted to his parents that he had a problem and they made sure he received medical help. Michael was an alcoholic.

Because of his poor choices, he was caught in his evil ways. His sins were like a rope that tied him fast.

—What does sin do to us if we don't confess it?

—What could Michael have done to avoid being caught in sin?

Further Reading: I John 1:9 (Reward your children if they memorize this verse.)

DAY 34

Proverbs 6:6 "Go watch the ants, you lazy person. Watch what they do and be wise."

THE VALUE OF WORK

Have you ever had a chance to watch an ant? You will never see one sitting around doing nothing. They are busy every minute building, hauling, or storing food. Ants never go hungry or go without shelter. They are hard workers, therefore their needs are met.

People can learn a lot from ants. Too often we concentrate on having fun or making ourselves happy instead of working hard. Of course, there are those who cannot work because of some physical disability but most of us are without excuse. Working hard is part of God's plan for us. It is fulfilling because we know that we are providing for ourselves and those around us.

II Thessalonians 3:10 says, "If anyone will not work, he will not eat." Even if you are too young to have a paying job, it is important that you learn to work hard. Next time you're given a job, do it cheerfully, knowing you are pleasing God by working hard.

—What can we learn by watching the ants?

—Why is working hard so good for us?

Further Reading: Proverbs 5:6–11

DAY 35

Proverbs 6:12,14b "Some people are wicked and no good. They go around telling lies...They are always causing trouble."

THE ONLY WAY OUT

Marjorie always seemed to be in trouble. No one trusted her because she claimed to have everything and be able to do anything. They began to ignore her because they knew this wasn't true. If Marjorie said it, you couldn't depend on it.

Since people ignored her, she began to do more and more things to get attention. She acted up in class, made fun of other people in order to make herself look better, and picked on other kids so she'd feel more powerful.

One day a girl invited Marjorie to a club at her church. Marjorie went, grumbling the whole way, but after she was there a while, she began to notice a real difference in the people around her. The club leader took an interest in Marjorie and spent extra time telling her about the wonderful person of Jesus Christ.

Marjorie decided she wanted to follow this Jesus. She knew he was the only one who could undo the mess she had made of her life.

Today Marjorie still has problems, but they are getting better. Each day she lets Jesus have a little more of her bad habits to transform them into good things in her life. She found that Jesus is our only escape from ourselves.

—What was Marjorie's problem?

—Why was she always in so much trouble?

—What changed her?

Further Reading: Romans 3:22–26

DAY 36

Proverbs 6:16–17a "There are six things the Lord hates. There are seven things he cannot stand: a proud look…"

A PROUD LOOK

Henry didn't think he was better than everyone else; he knew it. Everything was easy for him. He got straight A's without studying, he did well at any sport he tried, and he had a knack for knowing how to wear the latest styles. The trouble was not with Henry's natural abilities, it was with the way he lorded it over everyone else.

If someone struggled with a math problem, Henry's annoyance was clear on his face. When John fumbled the football, Henry looked at him with disdain, making John feel terrible. And if someone had trouble mastering the latest styles, Henry wouldn't give them the time of day.

Our proverb says that the Lord hates a proud look. Henry should have been thankful for his abilities, seeing them as an opportunity to assist others who weren't as fortunate. Instead, he made them feel worse.

—Why is pride so destructive?

—Is any kind of pride good?

Further reading: Mark 7:20–22

DAY 37

Proverbs 6:16–17b "There are six things the Lord hates. There are seven things he cannot stand: ... a lying tongue..."

A LYING TONGUE

Have you ever been around anyone who lies all the time? It becomes hard to even be with such a person after a while because you can never count on what he or she says.

But what about a person who only occasionally tells a lie? That doesn't seem too bad, does it? What if a kid tells a small lie to keep from getting in trouble? That's only natural, right?

It's easy to begin thinking that a "little" lie is no big deal, but our verse in Proverbs tells us that God looks at lying differently than we do. Read Proverbs 6:16-17b again. How does God feel about lying? He hates it — he can't stand it! Pretty strong language!

God gives us rules for our own good. Have you ever told a lie and felt miserable afterwards? He knows that only as we are honest with others and ourselves will we be truly happy people.

—How do you feel when someone lies to you?

—How does God feel when you lie?

—What can help remind us not to lie?

Further Reading: Colossians 3:9–10

DAY 38

Proverbs 6:16–17c "There are six things the Lord hates. There are seven things he cannot stand: ... hands that kill innocent people..."

INNOCENT LIVES

Last century, terrible things were going on in our world. Many in the United States were killed simply because others didn't like the color of their skin. In Europe, Hitler killed millions just because they were Jewish. When the Christian church was new, thousands of Christians were thrown to the lions because of what they believed. Today, many people in other countries still die for their beliefs.

What should our attitude be toward such horrible atrocities? The same attitude God has — we should hate the shedding of innocent blood. It should make our stomachs turn and bring tears to our eyes, but most of all, it should make us pray.

By the power of our prayers, lives can be changed and wickedness can be defeated. In fact, prayer is the most powerful weapon we have. Use it often!

—What does God hate?

—How should we feel about the killing of innocent people?

—What can we do about it?

Further Reading: John 10:9–10

DAY 39

Proverbs 6:16,18 "There are six things the Lord hates. There are seven he cannot stand: ...a mind that thinks up evil plans, feet that are quick to do evil..."

GUARD OUR MINDS

If you ever listen to the evening news, you will hear stories of theft, murder, divorce, hatred, cheating, and injustice. Have you ever wondered how a person becomes like those we hear about in news reports?

Our verse in Proverbs gives us a clue. It says that one of the things the Lord hates is "a mind that thinks up evil plans." All bad deeds start in the mind. Before a person ever steals, kills, or cheats, he has spent a lot of time thinking about such things. He has fooled himself into thinking that life is unfair and therefore he can do whatever he wants to make things even.

Of course, the next step after thinking about evil is doing evil. When an evil thought goes through our minds enough times, it begins to seem normal instead of wrong so that we are more likely to do the evil deed.

So how do we keep our minds clean? By filling it with God and His Word. No one else can help us in our thinking except the only One who knows what is in our mind. Ask Him to fill your thoughts with good today.

—Where do evil deeds begin?

—How can we control our thoughts?

Further Reading: Romans 8:6

DAY 40

Proverbs 6:16,19 "There are six things the Lord hates. There are seven things he cannot stand: ...a witness who tells lies and a man who causes trouble among brothers."

THE FALSE WITNESS

Bob lived next door to a large family. One of the good things about that was that he was never lonely. There was always someone around to play with, tease, or talk to.

However, the trouble was that Bob was often jealous of how well the kids in this family got along with each other. Tim was his favorite and he wanted Tim to think that he was the greatest.

One day, he observed another neighbor in Tim's backyard. This boy picked up Tim's favorite baseball bat and slammed it against a tree. Seeing the bat splinter, he quickly dropped it and ran home.

When Tim came out, he began yelling at his little brother, assuming he had broken the bat. Bob watched silently, never telling the truth. He hoped secretly that Tim would rather be with him than his brother.

"There are six things the Lord hates. There are seven things he cannot stand: ...a witness who tells lies and a man who causes trouble among brothers."

—How is Bob like the one in our Proverb?

—Is withholding the truth the same thing as a lie?

—Why does God hate it when a man causes trouble among brothers?

Further Reading: Matthew 5:23–24

DAY 41

Proverbs 6:20–22 "My son, keep your father's commands. Don't forget your mother's teaching. Remember their words forever. Let it be as if they were tied around your neck. They will guide you when you walk. They will guard you while you sleep. They will speak to you when you are awake."

REMEMBER...

As a little girl, I was often faced with disappointments. If I ever complained to my father about how unfair life was, he would sit down and face me at eye level. Many, many times I remember him repeating the same words to me. "It is all right because hard things build character." That is all he would say, but those words have echoed back to me my entire life.

Even now when I face disappointments, I remember my father's words. And you know what? He was right! The hard things I have gone through have built, strengthened, and prepared me for life. Most of all, they have drawn me to Jesus Christ who is my strength.

—What are we to remember according to our Proverb?

—What good will it do us to remember our father's commands and our mother's teaching?

—How will their words guide, guard, and speak to us?

Further Reading: Proverbs 6:23

DAY 42

Proverbs 6:25 "Don't want her because she is beautiful. Don't let her capture you by the way she looks at you."

THE TRAP

I read about a young girl in South America who was given an American magazine. On the cover was a glamorous movie star who seemed to have no flaws. This young girl studied the magazine constantly, wishing she were as beautiful as the actress.

Finally after years of saving her hard earned money, she took it all to a plastic surgeon and asked him to make her look as much like the actress as he could.

What a sad story this is. Here is a young girl whom God made in His image, yet she could not see the good He had done, only that which dissatisfied her.

Our proverb warns us of the trap that beauty can be. Beauty can fool the observer at first glance. One who looks beautiful on the outside may be a very ugly person to be around. On the other hand, I know people who seemed homely to me at first meeting, but now are beautiful to me because of their loving hearts.

This proverb is a warning to both men and women. Worry about what is inside a person more than the outside.

—What was wrong with the way the young girl thought about herself?

—What kind of beauty does God care about?

Further Reading: I Peter 3:3–4

DAY 43

Proverbs 6:27-29 "You cannot carry hot coals against your chest without burning your clothes. And you cannot walk on hot coals without burning your feet. The same thing happens if you have sexual relations with another man's wife. Anyone who does so will be punished."

HOT COALS

If you watch TV, go to movies, read magazines, or even look at billboards, you will see or hear something that has to do with sexual relations between a man and a woman. Sometimes the things you will hear and see will be good; sometimes they will be bad.

The thing is, God made men and women to want each other in a sexual way. As soon as he made Adam and Eve, He set up marriage so that men and women would have a place to have sexual relations. This was good.

However, when men and women began to sin, they soon ignored God's plan for them. They began to have sexual relations with those to whom they were not married. This has brought heartbreak to many as they have felt betrayed because their mate was not faithful to them.

"You cannot carry hot coals against your chest without burning your clothes". This is what a sexual relationship outside of marriage is like. It destroys rather than builds.

Remember that God made sexual relations to be good. We need to keep it good in the marriages he gives us.

—Can sexual relations be good?

—When are sexual relations bad?

Further Reading: Proverbs 7:5–27 (Parents, you may want to use this devotional to share more with your children on this subject.)

DAY 44

Proverbs 6:30–31 "People do not hate a thief when he steals because he is hungry. But if he is caught, he must pay back seven times what he stole. It may cost him everything he owns."

STEALING

After God gave the Jewish people the Ten Commandments, he also gave them many other rules to follow. One of them concerned stealing. The law stated that if one stole something, he must pay back double what he stole. And if he couldn't do that, he had to be sold as a servant. It gave people some pretty good reasons not to steal!

Our proverb today talks about a person who steals because he is hungry. It shows us that even if people understand why we would steal, it gets us into so much trouble that it is just not worth it. The message to us is that no matter how good of an excuse we feel we have to steal, it is wrong and we will be punished if we do it.

—Why is it a bad idea to steal even if we think we have a good reason?

—If we really need something, what is a better way to get it than stealing?

—If we see others who are hungry, what can we do to prevent them from stealing?

Further Reading: Philippians 4:11–13

DAY 45

Proverbs 7:1–3 "My son, remember what I say. Treasure my commands. Obey my commands, and you will live. Protect my teachings as you would your own eyes. Remind yourself of them. Write them down in your mind as if on a tablet."

PRECIOUS TEACHING

Do you ever ask your mom or dad, "Do we have to have a devotional tonight?", or do you think it even if you don't say it? I'm sure even Mom and Dad feel that way at times but our proverb for today tells us exactly why we take the daily reading of God's Word so seriously.

If you see a ball coming straight toward your eyes, what do you do? Do you say, "Oh, I'll just ignore it right now and think about putting my arms up to protect them later." Of course you don't! You do whatever you can to protect them because your eyes are precious and irreplaceable. That is how we are to think about God's Word. His teachings are precious to us. Without them we would be living lost and aimless lives.

In fact, His Word is so important that God tells us to "write them down in your mind as if on a tablet." We need to hear something a lot of times before it becomes that familiar to us.

Remind yourself of these words the next time it seems hard to listen to God's Word.

—Why do we have a devotional time?

—What good does it do us to hear God's Word?

Further Reading: Deuteronomy 6:4–9

DAY 46

Proverbs 7:4 "Be good to wisdom as if she were your sister. Make understanding your closest friend."

YOUR CLOSEST FRIEND

Janet was the kind girl who got along with just about everyone. She had a lot of friends and an understanding father and mother. But like all people, Janet occasionally had problems with schoolwork or her home life. When things didn't go her way, she knew there were two people she could always talk to— her sister and her best friend.

"Be good to wisdom as if she were your sister. Make understanding your closest friend." There are two things here that God wants to be as important to us as our family and friends. Those two things are wisdom and understanding.

If we are wise and understand God and others, we will be truly prepared for life. We will be making good decisions and loving others in a special way. Our lives will blossom as God works His perfect qualities into us.

—What two qualities does God want us to have?

—How do we make wisdom and understanding as important as our family and friends?

Further Reading: Proverbs 8:1–6

DAY 47

Proverbs 8:7 "What I say is true. I hate it when people speak evil."

WHAT I SAY IS TRUE

Sam was at James' house one day, when James' mother began telling Sam how she believed that when people died that they would later be reborn as another person on earth. "Therefore," she said, "it doesn't really matter what religion we are because everybody gets another chance."

Now, Sam knew the Bible says that we die once and then we are judged as to whether we will go to heaven or hell (Hebrews 9:27). He also knew that Jesus Christ is the only one who can forgive our sins so that we can go to heaven (John 3:16). Therefore, thinking about what James' mother said, he decided that what she believed was evil because it wasn't true. He knew that if she didn't change her mind that she would go to hell. He began telling her the truth in the Bible so that she could have eternal life.

—Why does God hate it when people speak evil?

—How should we feel when others speak evil?

Further Reading: Hebrews 9:27, John 3:16 (Parents, take time to explain the gospel message to your children with these verses)

DAY 48

Proverbs 8:8 "Everything I say is honest. Nothing I say is crooked or false."

HONESTY

I have a friend who is known for always telling the truth. In fact, he seems unable to tell a lie. Once we even kept his wife's surprise party a secret from him because we knew he would have trouble acting like he didn't know about it.

Many have heard the stories that gave Abraham Lincoln the nickname, "Honest Abe". Wouldn't it be wonderful to be so honest that when people thought of us that would be the word that came to their mind?

Solomon declares in our proverb today, "Everything I say is honest. Nothing I say is crooked or false." This is the great thing we can know about God's Word. It is always true. We will never be led astray if we listen to Him.

—What does it mean to be honest?

—Whose words are always true?

—How can we become more honest?

Further Reading: Deuteronomy 32:1–4

DAY 49

Proverbs 8:10 "Choose my teachings instead of silver. Choose knowledge rather than the finest gold."

SOLOMON'S REAL TREASURE

When Solomon became king of Israel, God told him that he would give him anything he wanted. What would you do if God said that to you? Would you choose money, friends, fame, or something else along those lines? Do you know what Solomon chose?

He said, "God, you have been so good to my father, David. He obeyed you. He was honest and lived right. Now you have let me be king but I don't know how to rule these people. All I ask for is wisdom. Help me to know right from wrong so that I can be a good king."

The Lord was very pleased with Solomon's request. He made him so wise that the whole world then and still today speaks about the wisdom of Solomon. As we read all the proverbs that he wrote, we can see that he truly was a wise man. He knew right from wrong. We are learning from his wisdom at this moment! "Choose my teachings instead of silver. Choose knowledge rather than the finest gold."

—What was most important to Solomon?

—What is wisdom?

Further Reading: Proverbs 8:9–12

DAY 50

Proverbs 8:13 "If you respect the Lord, you also will hate evil. It is wise to hate pride and bragging, evil ways and lies."

RESPECTING GOD

Even as a young child, Marcy had a great love and respect for God. She sincerely enjoyed Sunday school and listening to Bible stories. Whenever she heard of someone being kind or generous, it brought her a special joy inside.

At school, during a party, a movie was shown that was filled with bad language and sexual ideas. As Marcy sat watching the movie, she began to be uncomfortable because she knew her parents wouldn't approve of the movie. Even more, she knew it couldn't be pleasing to God.

Finally, she told the teacher that she didn't want to watch the movie. The teacher let her go to the computer room instead. Later she found out that the teacher turned the movie off because she, too, felt it was not a good example for the children.

"If you respect the Lord, you also will hate evil." Do you love God enough to hate evil?

—What are some evil things around us?

—How can we learn to respect God?

—How does hating evil show that we respect God?

Further Reading: Romans 14:11–12

DAY 51

Proverbs 8:17 "I [wisdom] love those who love me. Those who want me find me."

TRUE LOVE

There was a time when Travis was struggling with what God wanted him to do. His family had just moved to a new town where he started junior high school. This particular junior high was much different than the school he had just left. There were not as many rules at his new school, and his friends attended a lot of social activities which he knew he couldn't in good conscience attend.

Every day after school, Travis would read his Bible and ask God to help him to be strong against things he knew were wrong. His parents offered to put him in a nearby Christian school, but he was just getting used to this school, so he didn't want to change.

At last his parents found a church where other kids his age felt as he did. As he made friends at church, they helped him find alternatives to the activities that were wrong. He knew God had answered his prayer. "I [wisdom] love those who love me. Those who want me find me."

—How did Travis love wisdom?

—What shows that he was wise?

Further Reading: Proverbs 8:14–19

DAY 52

Proverbs 8:20 "I [wisdom] do what is right. I do what is fair."

THE RIGHT STUFF

Jordan was a peacemaker. He was from a large family and he really couldn't stand to see people fight. At a birthday party, his friend, Frank, received a game. All of them wanted to play it right away. The problem was that only six people could play and there were seven at the party.

Frank thought that his sister should be the one left out which really made her mad. When a fight erupted between them, Jordan solved the problem by saying that he would sit out the first game if someone would give up his or her place so he could play the second game. One of his friends agreed, making everyone happy.

Jordan found out that to be wise, we need to do what is right and what is fair.

—How do you feel about people who are fair with you?

—How about those who are unfair with you?

—In what ways is God always fair with us?

Further Reading: Micah 6:8

DAY 53

Proverbs 8:22 "I, wisdom, was with God when he began his work. This was before he made anything else long ago."

THE ONE WHO KNOWS EVERYTHING

Long ago there was a powerful king. He was so powerful that he could make or destroy towns as he pleased. One day he decided to make a large city. Rather than plan it out, he asked his carpenters to build houses and businesses wherever they wanted to put them. He commanded many different workers to plant trees and flowers, bushes, and grasses in any place they chose. He even had sewers and roads built in any place the laborers felt they wanted them.

This sounds pretty ridiculous, doesn't it? Imagine what the world would be like if God had not used wisdom. But thank goodness he did use wIsdom. He not only used it, he created it.

We wouldn't even know what wisdom was if we didn't know God. So, the next time you need wisdom, go to the One who knows everything.

—How would you feel if you had to live in the city that the king in our story built?

—How does wisdom make our lives better?

Further Reading: Proverbs 8:22–31

DAY 54

Proverbs 8:35 "Whoever finds me (wisdom) finds life. And the Lord will be pleased with him."

THE LORD'S PLEASURE

Alicia was an orphan. Her only parent died when she was four years old, so she was sent to live in a state institution. Every day she prayed that someone would adopt her, but it wasn't until she was ten years old that a man and woman who wanted her to be their own took her home.

Alicia was one of the very lucky ones who came into a home that loved her dearly and offered her great love and security. In return, she worked hard at pleasing them, making every effort to do the right thing. She found that it is easy to obey someone who loves you a great deal.

"Whoever finds me (wisdom) finds life. And the Lord will be pleased with him." The reason we should want to be wise, obedient people is because God loves us. To please Him should be a natural response to His love.

—Why should we want to be wise?

—How does wisdom give us life?

Further Reading: Proverbs 8:32–35

DAY 55

Proverbs 9:6 "Stop your foolish ways, and you will live. Be a person of understanding."

UNDERSTANDING

Jo was fun loving and what you would call "the life of the party". She was quick to make friends and good at getting a lot of attention. Most people wished that they could be like her. But there was something most people didn't know about Jo.

What they didn't know was that Jo wanted everyone to like her so that she could always be the center of attention. If she was nice to someone, it wasn't because she cared for the person; rather it was so that they would think she was something special.

"Stop your foolish ways, and you will live. Be a person of understanding," our proverb declares. This is the lesson that Jo must learn. In fact, all of us can learn this. We need to be people who really care about God first and others next. This is how one becomes a person of understanding.

—What was wrong with the way Jo treated people?

—What kind of people does God want us to be?

Further Reading: Proverbs 9:1–6

DAY 56

Proverbs 9:8 "Do not correct someone who makes fun of wisdom, or he will hate you. But correct a wise man, and he will love you."

THE WISE ONE IS CORRECTED

Will grew up with two best friends, Bob and Mark. The three of them did everything together. At the first snow, they would all be building a fort, and on the first warm day, they could be found swimming.

As they neared high school, Will and Mark noticed that Bob was drifting far away from them. He wanted to be with the crowd that got drunk on weekends and watched X-rated videos. They decided that they had to talk to him.

However, when they expressed their concern about his behavior, he just laughed at them. "You two just need to loosen up and have some fun once in a while," was Bob's reply. No matter what Will and Mark said, Bob refused to listen.

The three are now grown men. Will is a teacher, and Mark, a businessman, but Bob has never been able to make his life count. He still gets drunk on weekends, which has cost him a marriage and a job. The sad thing is that he still doesn't listen.

—Why does a wise man want to be corrected?

—How could Bob have changed?

Further Reading: Psalm 141:5

DAY 57

Proverbs 9:10 "Wisdom begins with respect for the Lord. And understanding begins with knowing God, the Holy One."

KNOWING GOD

If you had a chance to meet the President of the United States today, would you be excited? What about your favorite movie star or recording artist? Meeting someone famous would be fun, but would we be better people because we met them?

We have a chance to meet with the most exciting person who ever lived, any time we want. Who is that person? Jesus Christ. How do we meet with Him? Whenever we talk to Him, sing His praises, or listen to Him teach us through His Word. The great part is that each time we meet with Him, we become more like Him.

Take advantage of His wonderful company often. After all, how many friends do you have that can always pay attention to you? Jesus is listening. Don't keep Him waiting.

—How can we meet with Jesus?

—Why would we want to meet with Him?

Further Reading: John 17:3

DAY 58

Proverbs 9:11 "If you live wisely, you will live a long time. Wisdom will add years to your life."

A LONG LIFE

I know two women, Becky and Candy. Becky is very careful about the food she eats, trying to put into her body only that which is healthy. She also gets regular exercise, plenty of sleep, and avoids alcohol.

Candy, on the other hand, lives on sweets, never goes to bed before midnight, dabbles in drugs and alcohol, and is terribly overweight.

Which of these two women do you think will live the longest? Our proverb today is a very practical one. It is telling us that besides all the reasons we have heard for living wisely, we also have a chance at a longer life. God honors wise people who have made good decisions. This doesn't mean life will be problem free, but it does mean we can avoid a lot of unnecessary pain.

—What are some practical ways that you can live more wisely? Talk these over with Mom or Dad today.

Further Reading: Titus 1:15–16

DAY 59

Proverbs 9:13 "Foolishness is like a loud woman. She does not have wisdom or knowledge."

FOOLISHNESS

Roberta was Jane's mom. Whenever I went to her house, she was always complaining about something. She complained about Jane and her brother. She complained about the weather and her house. She even complained about herself!

"Foolishness is like a loud woman. She does not have wisdom or knowledge." Roberta was loud and also foolish. She drove everyone away from her, even though what she really wanted was friendship. If she had let Jesus change her attitude, she would have been a pleasant, rather than a bitter, person to be around.

We need to be careful with our attitudes. We should continually be trusting Jesus to change the poor way that we think about things or we will end up being foolish.

—Why was Roberta foolish?

—How is foolishness like a loud woman?

—How does a foolish person change?

Further Reading: Proverbs 9:13–18

DAY 60

Proverbs 10:1b "A wise son makes his father happy. But a foolish son makes his mother sad."

TWO SONS

Neil and Ron were brothers. Even though they were in the same family, they were quite different. Neil was very thoughtful of others and responsible in any task he was given. Ron tended to be more selfish and could not be trusted with even the smallest task because he just wouldn't do it.

As they grew, their basic characters continued as they were. Neil became a good husband and father who provided well for his family. Ron went through several divorces and jobs, bringing heartbreak to many.

Needless to say, Neil brought his parents a lifetime of happiness. Ron, on the other hand, brought them continuous sorrow.

How wonderful to be as wise as Neil was when we are young so that we can live a meaningful life.

—How was Neil wise?

—How was Ron foolish?

—What was the result in their lives?

Further Reading: Ephesians 6:1

DAY 61

Proverbs 10:2 "Riches gotten by doing wrong have no value. But right living will save you from death."

FALSE RICHES

A well-known actress told the talk show host the story of her life. "When I was new in Hollywood," she said, "I didn't have much choice in the parts that I could play. I had to take whatever I could get. I must admit that the movies I played in were really terrible. I'm ashamed of them, but that's the price you have to pay in order to become famous."

She went on to say that every role, no matter how bad, was worth it because it had brought her from poverty to great riches.

"Riches gotten by doing wrong have no value. But right living will save you from death." What this actress didn't understand is that someday she will have to face God and explain everything she ever did. Her great riches will mean nothing then.

—What did the actress think was important?

—What does God think is important?

—How could this actress change?

Further Reading: Psalm 49:7–10

DAY 62

Proverbs 10:3 "The Lord does not let people who live right go hungry. But he does not let evil people get what they hunger for."

FOOD THAT SATISFIES

There were two girls who both lived in the same town. One was very rich and had everything she could possibly want — a beautiful house, the latest clothes, every electronic device imaginable, and lots of great food.

The other girl had very little, other than the most basic food and enough clothes to get through until laundry day.

The funny thing was that the rich girl never was happy. No matter how much she had, there was always something more she wanted. She was selfish and, in spite of her wealth, had few friends.

The other girl loved everyone, which drew others to her. Even when her parents couldn't afford to buy her clothes, someone would give her what she needed just when she needed it most.

—Which girl do you think was more blessed by God?

—Why are evil people never satisfied?

Further Reading: Psalm 112:9–10

DAY 63

Proverbs 10:4 "A lazy person will end up poor. But a hard worker will become rich."

LAZINESS

Nick had trouble getting anything done. During his early years of school, he wasted time in class and failed to complete assignments. When in junior high school, he took a paper route because he wanted extra money, but he usually got the papers to the houses late and failed to collect money for them. While his friends took summer jobs, Nick just spent his time playing video games and watching television. Upon graduating from high school, Nick got a factory job but missed so many days of work that he was fired.

Nick was a lazy person. He was never able to make ends meet because he wouldn't do the work necessary to hold a job.

—What can you be doing now to make sure you are not lazy?

—Name two things that you work hard at.

—Name one thing at which you could be working harder.

Further Reading: 2 Thessalonians 3:10–13

DAY 64

Proverbs 10:7 "Good people will be remembered as a blessing. But evil people will soon be forgotten."

GOOD OR EVIL

The story is told of a woman during World War II who was held in a Nazi prison. She was arrested because she was hiding Jewish people from Hitler.

During her time in prison, she went through a great deal of suffering. One particular guard was especially mean to her, but she prayed for this guard and returned kindness for cruelty.

After the war, this woman gave her life to telling others that Jesus' love is greater than Satan's hate. She became known around the world and loved by many. No one ever heard from the cruel guard after the war. "Good people will be remembered as a blessing. But evil people will soon be forgotten." What a privilege to be a blessing to others.

—Can you name someone good who has been a blessing in your life?

—In what ways would you like to be like this woman who was a prisoner?

Further Reading: Hebrews 12:1–3

DAY 65

Proverbs 10:8 "A wise person does what he is told. But a talkative fool will be ruined."

DEEDS OVER WORDS

Jonathon is the kind of person you would call responsible. His parents often put him in charge of his younger brother because they knew he would take good care of him. Jonathon also had a lot of freedom because his family was confident that he would obey their rules even when he wasn't around them.

Janice, on the other hand, was always quick to volunteer to baby-sit her little brother, but whenever she did, something disastrous would happen because she would spend all her time on the phone or watching television instead of paying attention to her brother. Janice also complained continually that her parents never let her do anything. However, her mother knew that as soon as Janice was out of their home, she ignored all the family's rules and did as she pleased.

"A wise person does what he is told. But a talkative fool will be ruined."

—How did Jonathon show that he is wise?

—How did Janice demonstrate her foolishness?

—If you were a parent, who one would you trust?

Further Reading: Matthew 7:24

DAY 66

Proverbs 10:9 "The honest person will live safely. But the one who is dishonest will be caught."

AN HONEST MAN

Mr. Thompson is the most honest man I know. I remember being with him once at a restaurant that had a special discount for children under the age of twelve. I happened to be thirteen at the time, but I looked much younger. When the waitress brought Mr. Thompson the check, she charged me a child's price. It would have been an easy way for him to get out of paying so much money. No one would have known. But Mr. Thompson was an honest man. He never wanted anything false on his con-science. He immediately told the waitress that I was thirteen and that he would pay the full amount.

I learned a valuable lesson from Mr. Thompson. Anytime I feel like cheating someone just a little bit, I remember his example. "The honest person will live safely. But the one who is dishonest will be caught."

—Why is it so important to be honest?

—What is wrong with cheating just a little bit?

Further Reading: Luke 8:15

DAY 67

Proverbs 10:11 "Like a fountain of water, the words of a good person give life. But the words of the wicked contain nothing but violence."

WORDS OF LIFE

Everyone loved being with Dawn, who was an encouraging person. If a task seemed difficult, she would confidently state that she thought you could do it. If you were sad, she expressed sorrow, too, so that you knew she really cared. When you were excited about something, she would be just as excited as if it were happening to herself. Dawn was especially nice to be around when you felt like doing something wrong. She would gently remind you that God had better plans for you, making the wrong thing seem very silly indeed.

Dawn's words truly were like a fountain of water. They refreshed and renewed everyone around her.

—Can someone have life-giving words when they are not good people? Why not?

—How can words be like a fountain of water?

Further Reading: James 3:7–12

DAY 68

Proverbs 10:12 "Hatred stirs up trouble. But love forgives all wrongs."

THE POWER OF LOVE

Monty and Phil were good friends but one day at school, Phil overheard Monty telling a group of boys that Phil was a chicken. The two of them had gone to the fair together the day before and Phil had been afraid to ride the roller coaster that went backward and upside down. Phil thought Monty understood how he felt, but Monty made fun of him behind his back.

For several weeks Phil couldn't bring himself to talk to Monty. And each day that went by, he began to be angrier and angrier, until he felt such hatred for Monty that he never wanted to see him again.

It all came to a head at church one day when Phil's teacher talked about forgiveness. Phil realized that he had let his friendship with Monty be destroyed because he wouldn't forgive him. That day Phil called Monty on the phone to explain his hurt and anger towards him, which had vanished as God replaced it with His love.

—How does hatred stir up trouble?

—How can we love someone who has hurt us?

Further Reading: I Peter 4:8

DAY 69

Proverbs 10:14 "Wise people don't tell everything they know. But a foolish person talks too much and is ruined."

CLOSING OUR MOUTH

Jonna and Marsha were in the same Sunday school class, but they were very different girls.

Whenever the teacher would ask a question, Marsha's hand always went up. Often when the teacher called on her, she would make up an answer even if she didn't understand the question.

Jonna, on the other hand, was very thoughtful when asked a question. If she gave an answer, you knew that she was very sure that it was the right one.

After a while, the kids paid no attention at all to Marsha because they never really trusted what she had to say.

However, they all respected Jonna, fighting to sit by her, and anxious that she be on their team in any class competition.

—Why can listening be a lot more important than telling?

—How can talking too much ruin your reputation?

Further Reading: James 1:19, James 3:2

DAY 70

Proverbs 10:15–16 "Having lots of money protects the rich. But having no money destroys the poor. Good people are rewarded with life. But evil people are paid back with punishment."

THE END RESULT

Jesus tells a story in Luke, chapter 16, that explains what is really important in life. This is what he says:

"There was a rich man who always dressed in the finest clothes. He lived in luxury every day. There was also a very poor man named Lazarus, whose body was covered with sores. Lazarus was often placed at the rich man's gate. He wanted to eat only the small pieces of food that fell from the rich man's table. And the dogs would come and lick his sores! Later Lazarus died. The angels took Lazarus and placed him in the arms of Abraham. The rich man died, too, and was buried. But he was sent to where the dead are and had much pain. The rich man saw Abraham far away with Lazarus in his arms. He called, 'Father Abraham, have mercy on me! Send Lazarus to me so that he can dip his finger in water and cool my tongue. I am suffering in this fire!' But Abraham said, 'My child, remember when you lived? You had all the good things in life, but all the bad things happened to Lazarus. Now Lazarus is comforted here, and you are suffering. Also there is a big pit between you and us. No one can cross over to help you. And no one can leave there and come here.'"

After hearing Jesus' story, what do you think should be most important to us in our lives now?

—What did the rich man do wrong?

Further Reading: Luke 17:1–2

DAY 71

Proverbs 10:17 "The person who accepts correction is on the way to life. But the person who ignores correction will be ruined."

ACCEPT CORRECTION

Mitch is always in trouble. The other kids in his class always wonder why he never obeys the rules. Even as a small child, Mitch resented anyone who tried to tell him what to do. His own mother gradually quit trying to correct him and let him do as he pleased. The result was that Mitch is now always in trouble with somebody. He spends more time in the principal's office than he does in the classroom. Everyone, including his own classmates, is afraid that he will be in trouble his whole life.

"The person who accepts correction is on the way to life. But the person who ignores correction will be ruined."

—How could Mitch change for the better?

—How might ignoring correction ruin his life?

Further Reading: Hebrews 12:5–8

DAY 72

Proverbs 10:20–21 "The words of a good person are like pure silver. But an evil person's thoughts are worth little. A good person's words will help many others. But a foolish person dies because he doesn't have wisdom."

THE VALUE OF WORDS

Randy is the kind of person you would call inspiring. He spends his days in a wheelchair due to an automobile accident. You would think that Randy would become bitter because of his disability, but instead he is radiant. Even though he knows he will never walk again, he has a strong sense of God's working in his life.

"Before my accident, I was a very selfish person. But as a result of all the sitting around I had to do, I began spending a lot of time with God in His Word. I began to see that God was a lot more interested in my heart than in my legs. He's changing me into a person who cares more about others than myself."

Mick broke his arm during basketball season, putting him out of the starting line-up. Every day at school, he constantly complains about his handicap. Everyone is sick of hearing about it and wishes that Mick could think about something else.

"The words of a good person are like pure silver. But an evil person's thoughts are worth little. A good person's words will help many others. But a foolish person dies because he doesn't have wisdom."

—How did their accidents demonstrate the difference between Randy and Mick?

—Who would you rather be around?

Further Reading: Matthew 12:34–37

DAY 73

Proverbs 10:22 "The Lord's blessing brings wealth. And with it comes no sorrow."

TRULY WEALTHY

Mrs. Jamison loved being home with her children. She had three of them — two in school and one still at home. The trouble was that money was always tight. They seemed to always have just enough, but never any extra.

One day a businessman called, offering her a job as a secretary. It seemed the perfect solution at first, but as Mrs. Jamison thought about it, she saw some drawbacks. She would have to find a babysitter for her youngest child. She wouldn't be home when her children came home from school. She would never be able to enjoy her husband on his day off, which was in the middle of the week. The only thing the job really offered was money.

Proverbs 10:22 says, "The Lord's blessing brings wealth. And with it comes no sorrow." Mrs. Jamison decided that she was already as wealthy as could be.

—Can we be wealthy without having a lot of money? How?

—How do we get "the Lord's blessing"?

Further Reading: I Timothy 6:6–10

DAY 74

Proverbs 10:23–24 "A foolish person enjoys doing wrong. But a person with understanding enjoys doing what is wise. An evil person will get what he fears most. But a good person will receive what he wants most."

ENJOYING GOOD

Jeannie loved making life pleasurable for herself. She enjoyed it so much that it often became more important than anything else. Once at school, her teacher showed the class a beautiful stone that an uncle had polished for her. Jeannie wanted that stone.

During a study time later in the day, she found her opportunity. There was a long line at the desk filled with anxious students asking the teacher about a problem. While everyone was busy, Jeannie quickly slipped the stone into her pocket. However, she forgot that her pocket had a hole in it so the stone went through it and landed with a loud clattering on the floor. Jeannie was caught. Suddenly, life was not much fun since she spent many days staying after school.

—Why is it foolish to enjoy doing wrong?

—How can we enjoy doing what is wise?

Further Reading: Matthew 5:6

DAY 75

Proverbs 10:26 "A lazy person brings trouble to the one he works for. He bothers others like vinegar on the teeth or smoke in the eyes."

THE TROUBLE WITH BEING LAZY

A group of boys decided to earn money one fall by raking leaves. They all agreed that they would bring their own rakes and bags and charge according to the size of yard they were raking.

The first day, they all worked enthusiastically and earned a great deal of money. The people they worked for were pleased and recommended them to the neighbors. After a few days of working, a boy they called Dusty decided that there ought to be an easier way to earn money. He convinced the boys they should charge by the hour instead of by the size of the yard. The result was that they spent a lot more time goofing off when they should have been working. The cost was much greater for the people they were working for and they began to lose jobs. Soon no one wanted to hire them because of their reputation for laziness.

—What was wrong with Dusty's plan?

—How does one lazy person make it worse for everyone?

Further Reading: 2 Thessalonians 3:6–10

DAY 76

Proverbs 10:28 "A good person can look forward to happiness. But an evil person can expect nothing."

GENUINE HAPPINESS

Cindy had a rather hard life. She was sick a lot and had to move often because of her father's job. They were not especially rich, although they had everything they really needed.

Josie had a peaches-and-cream life. Her dad was wealthy and had lived in the same community since he was a small child. She had the same friends that she had always had, lived in a beautiful home, and had just about everything you could think of to buy.

But Cindy had one thing that Josie didn't have. She knew Jesus Christ and loved him wholeheartedly. She knew that life was not the greatest here on earth, but that Jesus had a place for her in heaven that was better than anything any of us could imagine. This expectation carried Cindy through a lot of days that Josie pouted through because she couldn't buy the new dress she wanted.

—Which girl do you think had the best reason to be happy?

—Why would Cindy's happiness be more lasting?

Further Reading: Proverbs 10:27–32

DAY 77

Proverbs 11:1 "The Lord hates dishonest scales. But he is pleased with correct weights."

HONEST SCALES

Audrey was entering junior high school and she wanted to earn some extra money to buy some new clothes. Her mother was having a garage sale so she gave Audrey permission to sell the popcorn seeds which they had grown in their garden. She gave her a scale to use, suggesting that she sell the seeds by the pound.

The popcorn sale was going very well but Audrey decided that she would have to sell an awful lot of seeds to buy the clothes that she wanted. She began putting her finger on the scale as she weighed the popcorn so that it would seem like her customers had a pound when they really only had three quarters of a pound. That way she would be able to get more money.

Audrey needed to read Proverbs 11:1, "The Lord hates dishonest scales. But he is pleased with correct weights."

—Why do you think God hates dishonesty?

—Why is cheating others so selfish?

Further Reading: Leviticus 19:35–37

DAY 78

Proverbs 11:2 "Pride leads only to shame. It is wise not to be proud."

DO NOT BE PROUD

Mike was very athletic. He always had been. He walked at nine months of age, was riding a bicycle at age four, could throw a ball directly over home plate by age seven, and rarely missed a free throw when he was ten. Mike was instantly successful at almost any sport he tried.

This would have been wonderful, but Mike wanted to make sure that everyone knew how great he was. He constantly bragged about how he led his team to victory. He belittled others who didn't find sports as easy as he did and told everyone in great detail about winning plays he made.

One day during an important basketball game, Mike made an unbelievable error. After the half, he grabbed the ball and ran to the other team's side of the court making a basket for them. It was a long time before Mike bragged about himself again.

"Pride leads only to shame. It is wise not to be proud."

—How does pride lead to shame?

—What would have been a better way for Mike to act concerning his ability?

Further Reading: I Corinthians 13:4

DAY 79

Proverbs 11:5 "The goodness of an innocent person makes his life easier. But a wicked person will be destroyed by his wickedness."

CHOOSE THE BETTER WAY

Jill and Marsha grew up as best of friends but somewhere along the line, their lives began to drift apart. Jill made choices that pleased God. She listened to His Word and to those around her who knew Him. As she entered adulthood, she married a man who also loved God and they served Him together.

Marsha decided that she wanted to live life her own way. She spent little time listening and even less time obeying God. She married a young man who enjoyed a good party much more than he cared for God or His people. After just five years, Marsha's marriage ended in divorce because she was unable to live with her alcoholic husband.

"The goodness of an innocent person makes his life easier. But a wicked person will be destroyed by his wickedness."

—How did Jill's goodness make her life easier?

—How did Marsha's wickedness destroy her?

Further Reading: Matthew 7:24–27

DAY 80

Proverbs 11:7 "When a wicked person dies, his hope is gone. The hopes he placed in his riches will come to nothing."

WHERE IS YOUR HOPE?

There was a man who grew up in poverty. Even the most basic things were hard for his family to come by. As he grew older, he vowed to never be poor again. He worked hard and used his shrewd business mind to build a great financial empire. Everyone who knew his story admired him because he had attained so much. He soon forgot what it was like to be desperately poor and did little to help those who were less fortunate, even despising them because they had not risen above their circumstances the way he did.

When this man was only fifty, he had a massive heart attack and died instantly. All his wealth went to others and he, in the end, had nothing.

"When a wicked person dies, his hope is gone. The hopes he placed in his riches will come to nothing."

—What was wrong with this man's attitude toward money?

—How could he have changed?

Further Reading: Luke 16:13

DAY 81

Proverbs 11:9 "By his words an evil person can destroy his neighbor. But a good person will escape by being smart."

SMART LIVING

An African-American family by the name of Smith moved into an all-white neighborhood. One of the white families was very upset about this and began spreading lies about the new family. Several other people in the neighborhood then began to send the Smiths letters, threatening their safety if they stayed.

The Smiths loved God and wanted to love their neighbors too. They began to visit the families around them, taking them goodies they had baked and offering to help them with some of their yard work. Soon the neighborhood overwhelmingly accepted the Smiths, instead shunning the neighbor who started the lies.

"By his words an evil person can destroy his neighbor. But a good person will escape by being smart."

—How can words destroy another person?

—How did the Smiths turn this bad thing into a chance to do good?

Further Reading: Matthew 22:34–40

DAY 82

Proverbs 11:11 "The influence of good people makes a city great. But the wicked can destroy it with their words."

GOOD INFLUENCES

In the middle 1800s, a community was begun by a group of people who had traveled west together. These people wanted to start a community that was founded upon God's principals. Of course, over time, others moved into the town who did not care about God, but the influence of the original people who settled the town was so strong that they continued to be a town that overall honored God. There were many times that it seemed difficult to speak against godless people, but those who were good remained firm in their convictions.

Today, we too can make a difference in the cities we live in. God's people must speak out for Him or we will become godless in all our ways. "The influence of good people makes a city great. But the wicked can destroy it with their words."

—Name some practical ways that we can help our communities to become godly.

Further Reading: Matthew 5:14–16

DAY 83

Proverbs 11:13 "A person who gossips can't keep secrets. But a trustworthy person can keep a secret."

THE GOSSIP

Melanie was planning a surprise party for her good friend, Zee. She wanted to invite all of Zee's closest friends so she began to call them, warning them to keep it a surprise. As she was deciding who to invite, she thought of Carmen. Carmen was a good friend of Zee's but she also knew that Carmen was a big gossip. She could never keep any information to herself. Melanie finally decided not to call her for fear that she would give the surprise away. Fortunately, this time Carmen's mouth only kept her from a fun activity. Her gossip often caused a lot of trouble.

"A person who gossips can't keep secrets. But a trustworthy person can keep a secret."

—Why didn't Melanie want to call Carmen?

—What is a "trustworthy" person?

Further Reading: Proverbs 20:6

DAY 84

Proverbs 11:14 "Without leadership a nation will be defeated. But when many people give advice, it will be safe."

GOOD ADVICE

Those who first founded the constitution of the United States of America must have understood Proverbs 11:14. They had all come from countries where kings ruled as they pleased, often causing great poverty and persecution for those they ruled.

The first Americans often knew their Bibles and had a great respect for God. Because of this, we have the great privilege of freedom. The system we live under is one in which everyone has a chance to speak about issues. Our job as Christians is to make sure we are speaking out about things that are important to God.

"Without leadership a nation will be defeated. But when many people give advice, it will be safe."

—Why is it important that Christians speak out for what they believe?

—Name some things that have changed in our nation because people spoke out.

Further Reading: Proverbs 15:22

DAY 85

Proverbs 11:15 "Whoever guarantees to pay what somebody else owes will suffer. It is safer to avoid such promises."

WISE STEWARDS

Vince came to our church with just a few dollars in his pocket. He had no job, had just suffered a divorce, and knew of no place that he could live.

Mr. Raymond befriended Vince, helping him to find a job and a place to live. After several months, Vince convinced Mr. Raymond to sign a loan for him so that he could buy a small house. For a while it looked like Vince was becoming responsible, but one day he just disappeared. No one ever heard from him again. Mr. Raymond was left with the debt of Vince's house which he had trouble selling, causing him great financial loss.

Mr. Raymond had a good heart but he should have avoided someone else's debt according to our proverb.

—How could Mr. Raymond have helped Vince without taking on a debt?

Further Reading: Romans 13:8

DAY 86

Proverbs 11:17–18 "A kind person is doing himself a favor. But a cruel person brings trouble on himself. An evil person really gains nothing from what he earns. But a good person will surely be rewarded."

A REWARD OF KINDNESS

During the Japanese invasion of Korea in World War II, there was a man whose entire family was killed by the invading army. This man, of course, was heartbroken but very soon afterwards he became a Christian. Knowing Jesus Christ personally brought healing and hope to his life.

Sometime later, this man again met those who had killed his family. They were consumed with hate and fear, but he could love them in spite of what they did. He had the privilege of leading one of them to Jesus Christ.

Today this man has been key to thousands of Koreans becoming Christians. God used him to make Korea one of the most Christian nations on earth. "A good person will surely be rewarded."

—How does a kind person do himself a favor?

—How does a cruel person bring trouble on himself?

Further Reading: Colossians 3:12

DAY 87

Proverbs 11:19–21 "Those who are truly good will live. But those who chase after evil will die. The Lord hates those with evil hearts. But he is pleased with those who are innocent. You can be sure that evil people will be punished. But those who do what is right will not be punished."

GOD SEES THE HEART

If we watch the news or read the newspapers, it seems as if good people finish last. We constantly hear about innocent people being hurt or killed, or good people being cheated. It makes you wonder if anything in life is fair.

But our proverb today says that God sees everything differently than we do. We only see the outside of people; He sees the heart. He also knows how everything is going to turn out in the end. So even if it seems like the bad people in the world are winning the battle, God knows that those who love Him are going to win the war. Those He is pleased with will be rewarded, while people with evil hearts will be punished. So, no matter how bad life seems, God is on your side.

—Why do the bad guys seem to win sometimes?

—How can we make sure God is pleased with us?

Further Reading: Psalm 119:1–3

DAY 88

Proverbs 11:22 "A beautiful woman without good sense is like a gold ring in a pig's snout."

A BEAUTIFUL WOMAN

Angie was a spoiled child who always got what she wanted. As she grew up, she became a beautiful woman to look at. She knew she was beautiful and decided to turn her beauty into a way to make money. She became a model and an actress, often taking roles which revealed a lot of her beautiful body but nothing of her character.

When she was still a young woman, she was in a terrible fire. It left her beautiful body scarred and ugly. She lost all of her jobs because the only thing she had to offer was beauty and now that was gone.

"A beautiful woman without good sense is like a gold ring in a pig's snout." The fire only showed the world what was inside of Angie.

—What should Angie have concentrated on instead of just her beauty?

—How could she have used her beauty in a good way?

Further Reading: I Timothy 2:9–10

DAY 89

Proverbs 11:25 "A person who gives to others will get richer. Whoever helps others will himself be helped."

A GIVING HEART

Stewart was a generous person. He just loved to see other people happy. There was a time at school that another boy didn't have a winter coat. Every day he would show up for school in his tattered spring coat, even when the temperatures dipped below zero.

Stewart had two coats for winter so he asked permission from his parents to give one of them to this other boy. It gave Stewart great joy to see this boy in his warm coat.

A few months later after school, a gang of boys decided to pick on Stewart. Seeing no way out, he started to despair. Suddenly, the same boy he had helped appeared and called the gang away. Stewart's kindness was repaid.

"A person who gives to others will get richer. Whoever helps others will himself be helped."

—How does a person who gives to others get richer?

—What are some practical ways we can be more generous?

Further Reading: Proverbs 11:24–28

DAY 90

Proverbs 11:29 "Whoever brings trouble to his family will be left with nothing but wind. And a foolish person will become a servant to the wise."

NOTHING BUT WIND

Gilda just couldn't get along with her family. She and her mother were always arguing. No matter what her mother said, Gilda would always say the opposite.

As she grew older, things just got worse at home. Her mother grew tired of even trying to talk to Gilda. As soon as she was eighteen, Gilda moved out of the house into her own apartment. In order to pay for the apartment, she got a job in a factory. The trouble was that she found she couldn't get along with her supervisor at work any more than she could get along with her mother. Gilda lost her job and her apartment because she never learned to listen to others.

"Whoever brings trouble to his family will be left with nothing but wind. And a foolish person will become a servant to the wise."

—If we can't get along with our families, what does that tell us about ourselves?

—What could Gilda have done differently to learn how to get along with her mother?

Further Reading: Luke 15:11–24

DAY 91

Proverbs 11:30 "As a tree makes fruit, a good person gives life to others. The wise person shows others how to be wise."

GIVE LIFE TO OTHERS

Jerry had a great family and a very good church. He had learned from the very beginning of his life that knowing Jesus is the most important thing a person can do.

It bothered Jerry that a lot of his friends didn't know Jesus. Most of them had never been to church or had never owned a Bible. Jerry began to pray for his friends and look for an opportunity to tell them how much Jesus cared about them. His chance came on the long bus ride he took to school. Whoever he sat by would hear about how they could know Jesus Christ. Many of his friends decided that they wanted what he had. Several began to attend church club meetings with Jerry so that they grew in their new-found faith.

Jerry was like a tree that produces fruit. He gave life to others as he taught them to be wise.

—How did Jerry give life to others?

—How was he showing his friends how to be wise?

Further Reading: John 15:5–8

DAY 92

Proverbs 12:1 "Anyone who loves learning accepts being corrected. But a person who hates being corrected is stupid."

LOVE LEARNING

Michelle has a lot of trouble with authority. If her parents, a teacher, her swimming instructor, or anyone else corrects her, she becomes defiant, refusing to listen to them. As a result, it is difficult for Michelle to ever become better in any area of her life. The very people who could help her, she refuses to listen to.

"Anyone who loves learning accepts being corrected. But a person who hates being corrected is stupid." Michelle is being stupid by not allowing anyone to correct her. She has no love for learning because she cannot be taught.

—How can correction help us?

—Why is it sometimes hard to be corrected?

—How does knowing what Proverbs 12:1 says help us feel better about being corrected?

Further Reading: 2 Timothy 3:16

DAY 93

Proverbs 12:3 "Doing evil brings a person no safety at all. But a good person has safety and security."

SAFETY

Jack had a plan for making money. It would have been good if his plan had simply included his paper route, but it wasn't enough money to satisfy him.

He began to tell his customers that the monthly rate for the papers was going up, which was not true. Jack then pocketed the extra money. This brought him more money but he worried all the time about someone finding out about his deception.

Eventually someone did find out and he lost his paper route with the promise that he would never work for the city paper again.

"Doing evil brings a person no safety at all. But a good person has safety and security." If Jack had done the right thing, he would have been worry-free.

—How does doing evil make us into worriers?

—How does doing good make us feel safe?

Further Reading: Deuteronomy 33:12

DAY 94

Proverbs 12:4 "A good wife is like a crown for her husband. But a disgraceful wife is like a disease in his bones."

A CROWN OR A DISEASE?

Jon and Ray both married at about the same time. Jon's wife has been a joy to him. She eagerly supports him in his work and constantly builds him up, telling him she believes in him. And she listens to his feelings, trying very hard to understand him.

Ray's wife, on the other hand, has been a constant thorn in his side. She nags him continually. No matter what he does for her, it's never good enough. If he tries to tell her how he feels, she belittles him for being weak.

Our proverb today is a lesson to men and women alike. Men need to look for a wife who will encourage them and women need to be the kind of wives who build up their husbands rather than tear them down.

—How is a good wife like a crown?

—How is a disgraceful wife like a disease in her husband's bones?

—What about the other way around? What would make a good or bad husband?

Further Reading: Ephesians 5:33

DAY 95

Proverbs 12:5 "The plans that good people make are fair. But the advice of the wicked will trick you."

WICKED ADVICE

The Packer family had worked hard all their lives to save money for retirement and their children's education. After years of saving a considerable amount, they met a man who said that he could double their money in just a couple of years. He spent a lot of time with the family and they were really convinced that he cared about them. So they gave him their entire savings and he vanished forever. They never heard from him again or ever saw their money again.

"The plans that good people make are fair. But the advice of the wicked will trick you." Jesus warns us in the New Testament that we are to be as "shrewd as serpents but as innocent as doves". We must be careful to let our minds make our decisions instead of our emotions.

—How can we learn to tell if someone is wicked or good?

—Why should we never listen to the advice of a wicked person?

Further Reading: Matthew 10:16–17

DAY 96

Proverbs 12:6 "The words of the wicked lie in wait for blood, but the mouth of the upright will deliver them."

DELIVERANCE

Years ago I heard the story of a woman who was walking home at night. As she was nearing her home, a man jumped out at her from behind a bush. She knew no one was around to protect her. No one except God.

She raised her voice loudly, "Get away from me Satan, in Jesus' name!" The man looked surprised, then turned and fled. Whether he thought she was crazy or whether one of God's angels came to defend her doesn't matter. What does matter is that this woman put her trust in God and He delivered her.

"The words of the wicked lie in wait for blood, but the mouth of the upright will deliver them."

—How do wicked people want to ruin our lives?

—How does God take care of people who love Him?

Further Reading: John 10:7–10

DAY 97

Proverbs 12:7 "Wicked people die and leave nothing behind. But a good man's family goes on."

HERITAGE

In the seventeenth century, two men chose their way in life. One chose to be a minister, sharing God's Word with those around him. The other chose a life of crime. He became a thief and spent many years in jail.

The interesting thing is what happened to these men's children, grandchildren, great grandchildren, and so on. The family of the minister followed in his footsteps becoming ministers, doctors, and lawyers. The family of the thief also lived lives of crime, many spending time in prison.

What our proverb tells us today is that the decisions we make now will not only affect our own lives, but also the lives of our children, grandchildren, and so on. Now is the time to begin living a godly life.

—How does the way we live affect our families?

—How will the decisions you make now affect your grandchildren?

Further Reading: Acts 24:15

DAY 98

Proverbs 12:8 "A wise person is praised. But a stupid person is not respected."

RESPECTED WISDOM

I was once in a group of girls who studied the Bible together. There were a lot of us in the group but I especially remember Kathy and Shelly. Kathy spent a lot of time reading and studying the Bible. As a result, we all wanted to listen to what she had to say when we read a passage. She almost always helped us understand the Bible better.

Shelly, however, often missed our Bible study. Even when she did come, she hadn't studied our passage so she knew little about it. Instead of sitting quietly and learning from others, she would give her own opinion, which usually just confused all who were there. Everyone dreaded her speaking.

"A wise person is praised. But a stupid person is not respected."

—What made Kathy respected in our story?

—Why was Shelly seen as foolish or stupid?

Further Reading: 2 Timothy 3:14–15

DAY 99

Proverbs 12:9 "A person might not be important but still have a servant. He is better off than someone who acts important but has no food."

PRIORITIES

Wyatt came from an interesting home. Everyone knew that his mom had a maid who lived with them. It was not that they were particularly rich, but they used their money for a maid because his mother had arthritis so severely that she couldn't keep up with the housework.

Barney's family had once been very rich because his dad won the lottery when Barney was a little boy. But his father was a gambler and spent far more money than he won, so they went from riches to rags as Barney grew older. Barney never waned to admit the fact that they were once again poor so he boasted of trips they were going to take and things they would buy even though he knew it wasn't true.

"A person might not be important but still have a servant. He is better off than someone who acts important but has no food."

—Would you rather be like Wyatt or like Barney? Why?

—Can you think of another way this proverb might be true?

Further Reading: I John 2:16

DAY 100

Proverbs 12:10 "A good man takes care of his animals. But even the kindest acts of the wicked are cruel."

COMPASSION

Betty wanted a cat more than anything in the world. Her parents finally agreed providing that she would take care of it. The cat would be entirely her responsibility. At first she did a good job feeding it, cleaning its litter box, and calling it in for the night. But after a few months, she got tired of the daily care her cat required. She started to forget to feed it daily and sometimes the cat wouldn't get water for days. During a particularly cold spell, she left the cat out all night so that its ears and paws were frostbitten. Soon her parents made her give the cat away.

Our proverb today lets us know that a good person will have compassion even on an animal, but a wicked person cares about no one.

—What did Betty do wrong?

—Why should we care what happens to animals that are in our care?

Further Reading: Matthew 10:29–31

DAY 101

Proverbs 12:11 "The person who works his land will have plenty of food. But the one who chases useless dreams isn't wise."

USELESS DREAMS

Zach and Willis both wanted to earn some money over the summer. Zach decided to get busy right away mowing lawns. He soon was doing seven lawns a week and earning quite a bit of money.

Willis didn't like the idea of getting all hot and sweaty mowing lawns so he came up with a new plan each week to earn money. He tried selling magazines for a week but soon he was sick of that. Then, he thought he would sell candy bars but never was organized enough to get any sold. Finally, he decided to take a newspaper route but that only lasted a couple of days. Soon the end of the summer arrived and Willis was broke.

—What was good about the way Zach earned money?

—What was wrong with the things Willis tried?

—What should our attitude be toward work?

Further Reading: Acts 20:34–35

DAY 102

Proverbs 12:12 "Evil people want what other evil people have stolen. But good people want to give to others."

STEAL OR GIVE?

"Psst," Amity whispered, "Colleen, how would you like to come over to my house after school? My uncle just brought home a bunch of jewelry from where he works. You can pick out whatever you want."

"Why did they let him bring it home?" Colleen asked.

"Oh, they don't know, silly!"

"You mean he stole it?"

"It's not really stealing, Colleen. I mean the factory makes tons of it. No one will miss it."

"But it is stealing, Amity. I couldn't take any of it."

Amity walked away shaking her head. She just didn't understand Colleen.

"Hi, Colleen!" Beth yelled across the schoolyard. "Would you like to come with us tomorrow night? We are going door to door in several neighborhoods to collect hats and mittens for the Salvation Army."

"I'd love to!" Colleen answered. "What time?"

—What was evil about what Amity wanted Colleen to do?

—What was good about what Beth wanted Colleen to do?

—How do you think God saw the three girls?

Further Reading: Proverbs 12:13–14

DAY 103

Proverbs 12:15 "A foolish person thinks he is doing right. But a wise person listens to advice."

FOOLISH DECISIONS

Max came to see Perry one afternoon while Perry was babysitting his little brother.

"Hey, Perry, there's a new video store downtown. Wanna check it out?"

"I'd like to, Max, but I've got to watch my little brother."

"Just bring him along. It's just a few blocks."

"Well... I need to call my mom at work and ask her if it's all right."

"We don't have time for that, Perry. Let's just go."

Perry finally decided to go but on the way they got in a hurry and his little brother had a bad fall and sprained his ankle. Perry ended up carrying him home and trying to explain the whole thing to his angry mother.

"A foolish person thinks he is doing right. But a wise person listens to advice."

—What should Perry have done before leaving the house?

—Why is it important to listen to advice?

Further Reading: Psalm 73:24–25

DAY 104

Proverbs 12:16 "A foolish person quickly shows that he is upset. But a wise person ignores an insult."

IGNORE AN INSULT

Clare is known for her terrible temper. One day a new girl in the school criticized Clare's hairstyle. Clare immediately lost her temper and the chance of ever having this girl for a friend.

Anne was just the opposite of Clare. She could laugh at herself and make people like her because of her good nature. During reading class one morning, Anne's words got all mixed up as she read aloud. Several of the other kids laughed and made fun of her but Anne just laughed along with them. Anne was very pleasant to be around.

"A foolish person quickly shows that he is upset. But a wise person ignores an insult."

—Why is it foolish to show our tempers quickly?

—Do you think it might be better to ignore an insult? Why or why not?

Further Reading: Ephesians 4:31–32

DAY 105

Proverbs 12:18 "Careless words stab like a sword. But wise words bring healing."

CARELESS WORDS

"Why don't you ever comb your hair, Emily? You always look like you've been through a war," laughed Crystal. Crystal knew Emily had a hard life since her mother had died when she was very young. Emily did much more work at home than most girls her age. Emily sadly hung her head at Crystal's words and unexpectedly burst into tears. Crystal looked shocked but instead of apologizing for her words, she just defended herself. "What's the big deal?" she said. "I didn't mean anything!"

Becky frowned at Crystal and put her arm around Emily. "Listen, Emily. You're one of the most beautiful people I know because you always want to do the right thing. I think I know a hairstyle that would look great on you. Do you want to do each other's hair?"

Emily dried her tears and smiled eagerly.

—How do careless words stab like a sword?

—Has that ever happened to you? If so, when?

—Why did Becky's words to Emily bring healing?

Further Reading: Psalm 56:9–11

DAY 106

Proverbs 12:19 "Truth will last forever. But lies last only a moment."

FLEETING LIES

"Warren, are you going to the game after school today? I'll sit with you."

"I thought you were grounded, Sam."

"I am but I just told my folks that I had to stay after school to do some make-up work. They believed me! Isn't that great?"

"I don't think it's so great, Sam. If you get caught, you're dead!"

"If I don't get caught, who's the worse for a little white lie?"

"You are, Sam. You are getting used to lying and that's a bad habit. Besides, God knows."

"What does He care?"

"He cares a lot. It says in Proverbs that 'Truth will last forever. But lies last only a moment.' When you meet God face to face, you are going to wish you stuck to the truth."

—How does truth last forever?

—Why does God care whether or not we tell the truth?

Further Reading: Isaiah 40:8; Proverbs 12:20–23

DAY 107

Proverbs 12:24a "Hard workers will become leaders."

A HARD WORKER

Wayne and Lyle grew up in the same neighborhood. Wayne always worked hard in school and during the summers at his various jobs. Lyle neglected his schoolwork and spent his summers driving around in his sports car.

When they were grown, they found themselves working for the same company. Wayne was vice president of the company, guiding the future of many of his coworkers. Wayne hired Lyle as a janitor. It was Lyle's last chance to prove that he could work hard. He had been fired from three previous jobs because of his laziness.

"Hard workers will become leaders."

—What good does hard work do us?

—How does laziness harm us?

—What could you do to learn to work harder?

Further Reading: Proverbs 12:27

DAY 108

Proverbs 12:25 "Worry makes a person feel as if he is carrying a heavy load. But a kind word cheers up a person."

A KIND WORD

Olivia's mother was sad a lot these days. She had lost her job and was afraid that they were going to lose their house. Each day when Olivia came home from school, her mother would shake her head "no" to tell her that she still hadn't found a job.

Her mother's worries made Olivia sad too, but one day she decided she was going to do what she could to make things better for her mom.

She began by writing her mom a letter. She told her what a great mom she was and how she knew she would get a job sooner or later. She even told her that it didn't matter if they lost their house as long as they were together. She reminded her mother of God's perfect love for her. For the first time in weeks, Olivia's mother smiled.

—Why is worry like a heavy load?

—How do kind words make the load lighter?

—Can you give an example of when a kind word made your load lighter?

Further Reading: Isaiah 50:4

DAY 109

Proverbs 12:28 "Doing what is right is the way to life. But there is another way that leads to death."

THE WAY TO LIFE

Jesus tells a story about the day all people will be judged. He says, "The Son of Man will come again in his great glory. All his angels will come with him. He will be King and sit on his great throne. All the people of the world will be gathered before him. Then he will separate them into two groups as a shepherd separates the sheep from the goats. The Son of Man will put the sheep, the good people, on his right and the goats, the bad people, on his left."

Jesus then goes on to say that those who love and obey him will receive the kingdom of God, prepared for them since the world was made. But those who don't love and obey him must go away from Him to be punished in the fire that burns forever. This fire was prepared for the devil and his helpers.

"Doing what is right is the way to life. But there is another way that leads to death."

—What is the way that leads to life?

—What is the way that leads to death?

Further Reading: Matthew 25:31–46

DAY 110

Proverbs 13:1 "A wise son takes his father's advice. But a person who hates being corrected is stupid."

DON'T HATE CORRECTION

"You'd better start working on your book report, Giles," Dad said as he noticed Giles was watching TV again.

"I've still got time, Dad. There are only a couple of chapters left to finish."

"Isn't it due Friday?"

"Yeah. I'll get it done. No sweat, Dad."

"Well, I'll tell you what. I will trust you this time, but if you don't get the book report done on time, no television for a month. Understand?"

"Yeah, I understand."

Unfortunately, Friday came and went but Giles never did get his book report done. When his dad asked him about it, he had no choice but to tell the truth.

"O.K., Giles," Dad replied. "I trusted you with your responsibility and you failed to fulfill your duty. I'm sorry, but no TV for a month. That was our deal, remember?"

Giles remembered. He wished he'd listened to his dad.

—Why should we take our parent's advice?

—Parents, share a time that you didn't listen to your parents that you regret.

Further Reading: Proverbs 13:2–4

DAY 111

Proverbs 13:10 "Pride leads to arguments. But those who take advice are wise."

ARGUMENTS

Lee was the kind of person who thought he knew everything. He argued with his parents. He argued with his friends. No matter what the subject was, he was sure that he was right. In fact, he loved arguing so much that he did so even when he knew he was wrong.

"Pride leads to arguments. But those who take advice are wise." Lee was so good at arguing and winning his point that it didn't matter anymore whether he was right or wrong; only that he won the argument. What Lee needed to learn was the benefit of listening to and learning from others. He needed to be concerned with truth more than persuasiveness. Lee must learn the difficult lesson of admitting when he is wrong and giving others credit when they are right.

—Why does pride lead to arguments?

—When should we take other people's advice?

—What other harm can pride bring?

Further Reading: Jeremiah 49:16

DAY 112

Proverbs 13:11 "Money that comes easily disappears quickly. But money that is gathered little by little will slowly grow."

EASY COME, EASY GO

Lois wanted to get a lot of money in a hurry. Her mother gave her a chance to earn money by helping around the house, but that seemed like too much work to Lois. So, she began to send in every sweepstakes entry that she could find. Finally after doing this for several months, she won $100.

It seemed like so much money to Lois. She went to the mall the Saturday after she received the money and spent every last cent. When the money was gone, she was not even sure what she ended up with for the money.

"Money that comes easily disappears quickly. But money that is gathered little by little will slowly grow." Perhaps if Lois had earned her money slowly, she may have been more careful how she spent it.

—What was wrong with Lois's attitude toward money?

—What is the proper attitude toward money?

Further Reading: Luke 16:11

DAY 113

Proverbs 13:12 "It is sad when you don't get what you hoped for. But when wishes come true, it's like eating fruit from the tree of life."

HOPES FULFILLED

Every weekend Sean's dad promised him that they would spend their entire Saturday together. He would talk about baseball games they would go to, or the fishing trip they would take, or the doghouse they would build. But every Saturday Sean's dad would have something come up at work so that none of their dreams came true.

After several years of these disappointments, Sean's dad had an opportunity to take a different job that left his weekends free. To Sean's delight, he and his dad went camping the very next weekend.

"It Is sad when you don't get what you hoped for. But when wishes come true, it's like eating fruit from the tree of life."

We all know what it is like to want something and be disappointed. Sometimes we have to be patient, perhaps even for years as Sean was, but often the waiting makes the fulfillment even more satisfying. Don't be afraid of the wait.

—Why is it like "eating fruit from the tree of life" to get what we hoped for?

—How should we handle it when our hopes are crushed?

Further Reading: Hebrews 6:18–19

DAY 114

Proverbs 13:14 "The teaching of a wise person gives life. It is like a fountain of water that can save people from death."

A FOUNTAIN OF WATER

One day as Jesus was traveling through a place called Samaria, he met a woman who was getting water from a well. He was thirsty so he asked her for a drink. Then he offered her "living water". The woman was immediately interested and asked him what he meant.

Jesus answered her, "Every person who drinks this water will be thirsty again. But whoever drinks the water I give will never be thirsty again. The water I give will become a spring of water flowing inside him. It will give him eternal life."

Our proverb today says that "The teaching of a wise person gives life. It is like a fountain of water that can save people from death." Jesus is that "fountain of water" for us. He's the only one who can give us eternal life.

—How is Jesus our "living water"?

—What kind of thirst does he quench in us?

Further Reading: John 14:6

DAY 115

Proverbs 13:20 "Whoever spends time with wise people will become wise. But whoever makes friends with fools will suffer."

CHOOSING YOUR FRIENDS

Carol became a Christian when she was nine years old. She really understood what she was doing and she loved Jesus very much. But when Carol entered junior high school, it seemed as though none of the popular kids were Christians. She wanted to be popular so she left all her Christian friends behind. It was not long before she was going to all the best parties and dances. She gave little thought to Jesus anymore and what He wanted to make of her life. Friends and fun were all the mattered.

Finally, when Carol reached high school, one of her old friends talked her into going to a Christian retreat. At that retreat, Carol realized that she had surrounded herself with all the wrong people and that she couldn't live the Christian life by herself. She renewed her old friendships at church and found out what a great group of kids they had become.

—Why do we become like those we spend our time with?

—How do we handle the longing to be popular above all else?

—What do you look for in a friend?

Further Reading: Proverbs 13:15–22

DAY 116

Proverbs 13:23 "A poor man's field might have plenty of food. But unfair people steal it from him."

INJUSTICE

I read a story about a woman whose husband died while she was in her fifties. They were poor people, but her husband did leave her their small house so that she at least had a place to stay.

Unfortunately, this woman didn't understand much about managing her affairs. She failed to pay her taxes for a few years after he died. Another man in town had found a legal but horrible way to make money. He would find out who was behind on their taxes, pay the taxes they owed, and take possession of their home. This was perfectly legal but terribly mean. This poor woman lost her only security, her house, because of this man's greed.

Our proverb today warns us against such injustice. We need to be careful that we are never part of such unfair practices.

—How can one person's greed hurt another person?

—Why should we be satisfied with what is our share?

Further Reading: Leviticus 19:11–16

DAY 117

Proverbs 13:24 "If a person does not punish his children, he does not love them. But the person who loves his children is careful to correct them.

A LOVING PARENT

"Why are you always so rough on me?" Carl exclaimed. "Mark's folks never ground him."

"You didn't come straight home after school like I asked you to do, Carl. It is very important that you do what I say in the little things or I'll never be able to trust you in the big things. I'm sorry, but you won't be going to anyone's house for a week so that you will remember to listen to me next time."

"It still doesn't seem fair!" Carl yelled.

"I care about what kind of person you become, Carl," his mother added. "It will make a difference to everyone around you when you are older if you are trustworthy."

"If a person does not punish his children, he does not love them. But the person who loves his children is careful to correct them."

—How could love and punishment go together?

—So why is it hard to be punished?

—Mom or Dad, share a time you learned a lesson from a punishment.

Further Reading: Deuteronomy 8:5

DAY 118

Proverbs 14:1 "A wise woman strengthens her family. But a foolish woman destroys hers by what she does."

A FOOLISH WOMAN

Mrs. Thompson and Mrs. Palmer were very different kinds of mothers. Mrs. Thompson spent a lot of time with her children, often did little things to surprise them, and made sure they were doing well in school.

Not Mrs. Palmer. She avoided spending any more time with her children than she had to, never did anything extra for them, and didn't even know what they were learning in school. Her only desire was to get rid of them as often as possible.

"A wise woman strengthens her family. But a foolish woman destroys hers by what she does." Mrs. Palmer was destroying her family by her neglect while Mrs. Thompson was strengthening hers by her concern.

—How does wisdom affect the kind of parents we will be?

—How does a person become foolish?

—How does a person become wise?

Further Reading: Ruth 1:16–17

DAY 119

Proverbs 14:2 "People who live good lives show respect for the Lord. But those who live evil lives show no respect for him."

RESPECT FOR THE LORD

Garret became a Christian at a big rally with a lot of other kids his age. It seemed like an exciting thing to do at the time. But as Garret grew older, he found it very hard to live the way the Bible says we should. Finally, he just gave up. He lived exactly as those who didn't know Christ lived — he drank, smoked, and experimented with drugs and sex. He showed no love for others unless he thought there was something in it for him.

One of his friends, who had remained in a close relationship with Jesus Christ, spoke with him about his life style.

"Hey, I'm saved. What difference does it make how I live?" Garret replied.

"It's like slapping God in the face, Garret." His friend went on to say, "If we can't even respect God enough to obey him, we certainly don't love him. If I were you, I'd make sure I was right with God and not just counting on a prayer I prayed years ago."

—How does living a good life show respect for the Lord?

—How does living an evil life show disrespect for God?

Further Reading: James 1:26–27

DAY 120

Proverbs 14:5 "A truthful witness will not lie. But a false witness tells nothing but lies."

A FALSE WITNESS

Cynthia and Erica were asked to run an errand together at school. They were to deliver a package from the office to the science room. Before returning to the room, Cynthia had to use the restroom. As Erica waited for her, she dropped the package. It landed with a sickening thud and the sound of broken glass. Fearing punishment, Erica handed the package to Cynthia to carry, not saying a word about dropping it.

When the teacher opened the package and found the contents broken, she questioned Cynthia about it. Cynthia honestly replied that she didn't know how it had happened. The teacher didn't believe Cynthia and wrote out a detention for her.

The following day, when the detention would be carried out, Erica went to her science teacher. She hadn't slept much the night before because she felt so guilty about Cynthia being punished for what she did not do. As she confessed the truth, the science teacher forgave her. The teacher had not been nearly as concerned about the package as she had about the lie.

—Why is it so important that a witness be truthful?

—What might happen if a witness is not truthful?

Further Reading: Revelation 1:4–5

DAY 121

Proverbs 14:6 "Those who make fun of wisdom look for it but do not find it. But the person with understanding easily finds knowledge."

THE ONE WHO KNOWS THE ANSWERS

"Why do you always go to church so much, Larry? It seems like a big waste of time to me. You don't need to use God as a crutch."

"I don't use him as a crutch, Max. He's more like a whole new pair of legs. He made you, Max. It might be worth your time finding out about Him."

Later that year, Max's dad died.

"I'm so sorry to hear about your dad, Max."

"Man, Larry, I wish I knew more about what happens to a person when he dies. I've been all torn up inside trying to figure out why this happened. Doesn't anybody have any answers?"

"I don't know all the answers, but I can help you get to know the One who does. He wants to help you right now, Max."

"Maybe you're right, Larry. Maybe."

—Why is it impossible to find wisdom without God?

—How do we become a "person with understanding"?

Further Reading: Ecclesiastes 7:12

DAY 122

Proverbs 14:9 "Foolish people don't care if they sin. But honest people work at being right with others."

BEING RIGHT WITH OTHERS

"I think I'll go talk to Marie and see what's wrong. She seems so sad today. I wonder if I said anything to hurt her feelings."

"Don't waste your time on her, Leona. She's so weird anyway. Let's go have some fun instead."

"I can't have fun if I keep seeing Marie's sad face. She's really nice if you'd give her a chance. She's just shy."

"I still think she's strange and I don't want anything to do with her. You can blow your free time on her if you want, but I'm sure not going to."

"What if others treated you that way?" Leona asked as she walked toward Marie.

"Foolish people don't care if they sin. But honest people work at being right with others."

—Why was Leona's attitude right and her friend's attitude sinful?

—Why is it so important that we be "right with others"?

Further Reading: Matthew 5:46–47

DAY 123

Proverbs 14:10 "No one else can know your sadness. Strangers cannot share your joy."

SADNESS AND JOY

Jessica started crying again. It had been so hard to move away from all her friends. Now she didn't know anyone. There was no one to talk to about how miserable she felt. Even when her dad brought her home a brand new stuffed bear, it didn't cheer her up for very long. She didn't even have anyone she could call to tell them about it.

So now she sat on her bed, flipping through her Bible. "Please God, I need help right now. Show me something to get me through this."

Suddenly she remembered a verse she had learned in Sunday school. She turned to the book of Jeremiah after finding it in her index. In chapter 31, verse 3, she found these words, "And from far away the Lord appeared to his people. He said, 'I love you people with a love that will last forever. I became your friend because of my love and kindness.'"

Jessica closed her Bible breathing these words, "Thank you, Lord. That will get me through."

—Who is the only one who can really understand our sadness?

—Why does it help to know that God understands and cares?

Further Reading: John 14:18

DAY 124

Proverbs 14:12 "Some people think they are doing what's right. But what they are doing will really kill them."

DON'T BE DECEIVED

"Linda, do you want to come with me to June's house tonight? We are going to have a séance."

"Isn't that kind of satanic or something?"

"Oh no, it's a way to get in touch with people you love who have died. It's really a good thing. Marsha got to talk to her great-grandmother last time we did it. She is acting as our medium to get in touch with our loved ones."

"I don't think so, Jewel. A séance is just a way to get in contact with the devil. My parent warned me about them."

"No. You've got to be wrong, Linda. Why would they tell you something like that?"

"Because it's true, Jewel. I wish you wouldn't go either. Why don't you come to my house instead?"

"I'm going to June's. I wouldn't miss it!" Jewel's eyes flashed in anger at Linda.

Linda walked away sadly, whispering a prayer for her friend.

—What was Jewel doing that seemed right to her?

—What was wrong with going to a séance?

Further Reading: Deuteronomy 18:10–13

DAY 125

Proverbs 14:13 "When someone is laughing, he may be sad inside. And when the laughter is over, there is sorrow."

SENSITIVITY

"I swear, Jasper, you get rounder every day. Where do you put all that food you eat?"

Jasper smiled and chuckled, "Oh, I just start filling up both legs when my stomach gets full."

"I know," added another kid, "we can enter you in the largest pumpkin contest at school."

"Good idea," laughed Jasper. "I'll just wear orange. It should be perfect."

Soon everyone tired of teasing Jasper and the kids started leaving the lunch table. Only he and Luke were left.

"Don't you want to make fun of me too, Luke?"

"Nope, I think it's rotten. Why do you put up with it?"

"What can I do? It's better to laugh about it. It sure gets tough sometimes though. I know I'm fat but I don't know what to do about it."

"Well, I'll never make fun of you, Jasper. You can count on that."

—How can someone be sad inside when they are laughing?

—What can we do to make sure that we don't laugh at something that makes another person sad?

Further Reading: Psalm 90:14–17

DAY 126

Proverbs 14:15 "A foolish person will believe anything. But a wise person thinks about what he does."

THINK IT THROUGH

"Do you want to come to the movies with us, Vic? We're walking to the theater after school."

"What are you going to watch?"

"That new show about the crazy cops who are always doing everything wrong."

"What's it rated?"

"I don't know. But it's all right. It's not a bad movie."

"O.K., I'll go. What about you, Jason?"

"Nope. I'll have to ask my parents. They're pretty particular about what I watch. They're always saying, 'You can't take something out of your mind once it's in there. It stays forever.' I know, they're weird, but what can I do?"

"You'll be sorry, Jason."

"Better safe, than sorry."

Our proverb today says, "A foolish person will believe anything. But a wise person thinks about what he does."

—Why was Vic foolish?

—Why was Jason wise?

Further Reading: Philippians 3:7–8

DAY 127

Proverbs 14:19 "Evil people will have to bow down to good people. The wicked will bow down at the door of those who do right."

EVERY KNEE SHALL BOW

We see evidence everyday of evil people bowing down to good people. When a murderer or thief is convicted of a crime, they in a sense "bow down" to a just system that punishes them for their crime.

But on a much greater scale, all evil and good people alike will bow to our Lord Jesus Christ. Philippians 2:9-11 says, "So God raised Christ to the highest place. God made the name of Christ greater than every other name. God wants every knee to bow to Jesus — everyone in heaven, on earth, and under the earth. Everyone will say, 'Jesus Christ is Lord' and bring glory to God the Father."

I don't know about you, but on that day when we all bow to Jesus Christ, I sure don't want to be one of the evil ones!

—Can you think of other ways that evil people bow down to good people?

—How does knowing that we will all someday bow to Jesus make a difference in the way we live now?

Further Reading: Revelation 5:11–14

DAY 128

Proverbs 14:20 "The poor are rejected, even by their neighbors. But rich people have many friends."

RICH OR POOR?

Wanda knocked at Valerie's door. "Hi. Let's go over to Rita's house again. They have more rooms than I can count, and I hear they just put in a new chandelier from Paris. I can't wait to see it."

"No thanks, Wanda. I'm going over to visit Mrs. Jones. She's so lonely."

"Ugh. You're going in that house? It looks like it's full of roaches."

"I'm sure she does have a few, but no one else visits her. She counts on me coming over on Thursdays."

"I don't get you, Valerie. You turn down Rita's house for Mrs. Jones' place?"

"Not exactly, Wanda. I'm turning down Rita for Mrs. Jones. Rita may have a lot of money but Mrs. Jones has a great heart. You ought to come with me some time and get to know her."

"No chance! I wouldn't be caught dead in that house."

—What was wrong with Wanda's attitude toward the poor? Toward the rich?

—How did Valerie show God's love to Mrs. Jones?

Further Reading: James 1:9–10; Proverbs 14:21–24

DAY 129

Proverbs 14:26 "A person who respects the Lord will have security. And his children will be protected."

PROTECTION

There is a true tale about a woman who lived in Holland during the Nazi invasion of that country. She was a God-fearing woman who wanted to please Him in all that she did.

When the Nazis came to her village looking for young men to serve in their armed forces, she became very worried about her teenage son. As the Nazis approached her house, she hid him under the floor in the cellar then she covered the spot with a rug and a table.

When the soldiers entered her house demanding the whereabouts of her son, she truthfully answered that he was under the table. Lifting the tablecloth, they of course, saw no one so they left her house, never to bother her again.

"A person who respects the Lord will have security. And his children will be protected." Even though our very lives may be threatened at times, we are the most secure people on earth because we know our Maker.

—What does it mean to "respect the Lord"?

—Why do people that respect the Lord have security?

Further Reading: Isaiah 33:6

DAY 130

Proverbs 14:30 "Peace of mind means a healthy body. But jealousy will rot your bones."

JEALOUSY

Lance and Keith had been good friends for a long time. When Keith received his driver's license, he was able to buy his uncle's sports car. It was in perfect condition and because his uncle wanted to help him out, he gave Keith a really good deal.

Lance loved Keith's car. In fact, he was convinced that he loved it more than Keith did. Every time Lance saw the car, he felt very jealous. It became so bad that soon he didn't even want to see Keith because all he would think about was how he wished he could have his car. His stomach began to tie up into knots when Keith walked into the room.

"Peace of mind means a healthy body. But jealousy will rot your bones."

—How was jealousy rotting Lance's bones?

—What could Lance have done to obtain peace of mind?

—Have you ever felt like being jealous "rotted your bones"?

Further Reading: Philippians 4:7

DAY 131

Proverbs 14:31 "Whoever is cruel to the poor insults their Maker. But anyone who is kind to the needy honors God."

BE KIND TO THE NEEDY

Mr. Oakland owned a lot of property in town. Most of his apartment buildings were in the poor section of town. When Mr. Lewis, a member of Mr. Oakland's church, rented an apartment from him, things went fine for a while. But then Mr. Lewis lost his job. He had three young children to support and just couldn't find another job right away.

The minister of their church went to see Mr. Oakland because Mr. Lewis couldn't afford to pay the rent. He asked Mr. Oakland to give him time to find a job before kicking him out of the apartment. Mr. Oakland refused, stating that Mr. Lewis must be doing something wrong if he couldn't find a job.

The minister left Mr. Oakland's beautiful home with thoughts of Proverbs 14:31 in his mind, "Whoever is cruel to the poor insults their Maker. But anyone who is kind to the needy honors God."

—How was Mr. Oakland insulting God?

—What difference does it make to God how we treat the poor?

Further Reading: Job 31:13–19

DAY 132

Proverbs 14:34 "Doing what is right makes a nation great. But sin will bring disgrace to any people."

A GREAT NATION

When a famous minister came to the United States from Europe in the middle 1800s, he made an observation. He said, "America is great because America is good. If America ceases to be good, it will cease to be great."

Solomon knew this as God inspired him to write the book of Proverbs, "Doing what is right makes a nation great. But sin will bring disgrace to any people."

Our nation has corrected many wrongs, but is plagued by many more. We have become an immoral nation, seeking pleasure over doing what is right. We also are obsessed with our own wealth and happiness. Unless Christians lead the way in turning to God and away from our sin, we will certainly cease to be a great nation.

—How does doing what is right make a nation great?

—How can Christians help a nation do what is right?

Further Reading: 2 Chronicles 7:14

DAY 133

Proverbs 15:1 "A gentle answer will calm a person's anger. But an unkind answer will cause more anger."

A GENTLE ANSWER

"Josie! Why did you tell Ivy that I was afraid of the water? What a mean thing to do! She has been making fun of me all morning. I trusted you when I told you and now you blab it all over school. I can't help it if I never learned how to swim."

"Take it easy, Gail," Josie replied calmly. "I only told Ivy because she was thinking of having a surprise birthday party for you — a swimming party. I knew you would be embarrassed if she did that, so I told her. I'm truly sorry that she used it to make fun of you. I never imagined she would do that."

"Oh gee, Josie. I feel awful. Will you forgive me for yelling at you?"

"Of course. What are friends for, anyway?"

"A gentle answer will calm a person's anger. But an unkind answer will cause more anger."

—Would Gail have acted differently if Josie had yelled back at her?

—Why was it so important to their friendship that Josie stay calm?

—How should we react when others are angry with us?

Further Reading: Ephesians 4:26

DAY 134

Proverbs 15:3 "The Lord's eyes see everything that happens. He watches both evil and good people."

GOD IS WATCHING

Ted kept looking at the video games. He wanted the new one that just came out but he didn't have forty dollars to buy it. The shopkeeper was busy with another customer. Who would know? He slipped the game into his jacket and walked out of the store.

Russ knew that Harvey didn't have any money to buy lunch with at school that day. He wanted to help him out without embarrassing him so he slipped some money into his locker when he wasn't looking. Harvey ate a good lunch that day but he never knew who to thank for it.

Why does it seem like people who do wrong sometimes get away with it? And people who are good often receive no credit for their good deeds? It may seem uneven but our proverb says, "The Lord's eyes see everything that happens. He watches both evil and good people." We need to remember that all punishment and rewards are not given right away. We may have to wait until we meet God but nothing goes unnoticed by Him. It matters what we do.

—What difference does it make in our behavior that God always is watching us?

—How can knowing that He is watching make us feel better?

Further Reading: Colossians 3:23–25

DAY 135

Proverbs 15:4 "As a tree gives us fruit, healing words give us life. But evil words crush the spirit."

HEAL OR CRUSH

"Elspeth! What a weird name. She must be stranger than she looks."

"Yeah, that is a different name, alright. I think she has a drawl too. She sounds funnier than anyone else I've ever heard."

Elspeth moved away from the door. The girls didn't know she was there as they continued to talk about her. Her heart felt so heavy. Never had she felt more alone than now. She moved on down the hall to the restroom. As she entered, she saw Clara combing her hair. She liked Clara but was afraid to talk to her after hearing what the other girls said.

Clara noticed her right away. "Hi, Elspeth. I just got this new perfume for my birthday. Would you like to try it?"

Elspeth raised her head with hope in her eyes. "I'd love to," she answered, trying hard not to drawl.

"You have the most beautiful voice, Elspeth. It has such a nice lilt to it. I love to hear you talk."

Elspeth smiled for the first time that day.

—How did the girls at the beginning of our story crush Elspeth's spirit?

—How did Clara's words heal Elspeth's spirit?

—What can we do to be careful what we say to and about others?

Further Reading: Philippians 2:5

DAY 136

Proverbs 15:8 "The Lord hates the sacrifice that the wicked offers. But he is pleased with an honest person's prayer."

AN HONEST PERSON'S PRAYER

When there was a great amount of people starving to death in the country of Ethiopia, many were concerned for them.

One who was concerned was a rock singer who had been noticing the Ethiopians on the news. He decided to put on a concert and then give all the money to help Ethiopia. Besides, a lot of people thought his music was a bad influence on kids. If he did something nice like this, they would probably change their mind about him and he would become more popular.

Another who was concerned for the Ethiopians was a poor man who lived on his social security checks. He knew that he could not help the Ethiopians in a physical way but he began to pray for them. He prayed in the morning when he got up and at night when he went to bed. Sometimes he even skipped his own lunch while he prayed and sent the few dollars he saved to a relief fund to help them.

"The Lord hates the sacrifice that the wicked person offers. But he is pleased with an honest person's prayer."

—Who do you think the Lord was pleased with in our story, the rock singer, or the poor man? Why?

Further Reading: I Samuel 15:22

DAY 137

Proverbs 15:11 "The Lord knows what is happening where the dead people are. So he can surely know what people are thinking."

HE KNOWS OUR THOUGHTS

Carlotta was bored. It was Sunday morning again and she had to sit in church. Mr. and Mrs. Charles were telling the congregation about the difference that Jesus Christ had made in their lives.

"He sure has a big nose," Carlotta thought to herself. "And Mrs. Charles always wears that same old dress. I can't believe I have to sit through the sermon next." Finally they got finished. "I thought they were going to talk forever. Oh no, here comes the minister. I'll bet he'll talk for forty minutes. Why can't he tell more jokes or something?

"Hey look over there! I've never seen that boy before. He's pretty cute. Maybe I can get him to notice me if we ever get this church service over with. If I stare at him long enough, he's bound to look this way. I wish church was over. When I'm old enough, I'm never coming to church again. Finally, it's over."

"Thank you for being so nice and quiet, Carlotta. What a good girl you are," Mrs. Kelly said as she patted Carlotta's arm.

—Read our verse again. According to that verse, why was Mrs. Kelly wrong about Carlotta?

—What was wrong with Carlotta's thoughts?

—How could she improve her thoughts?

Further Reading: I Corinthians 4:5

DAY 138

Proverbs 15:14 "Smart people want more knowledge. But a foolish person just wants more foolishness."

BE SMART

Conrad and Micah were in the same class at school. Micah was a hard worker. He used his study time to get his homework done and free time to read books or work on the computer. He loved to learn and even did so as he played games and talked to others. He wanted to know more about everything.

Conrad was just the opposite. He spent study time throwing spit wads, and free time pulling the girls' hair. Even when he talked to others, he refused to learn. He never listened very well to anyone. Conrad's only desire in life was to have fun any way he could get it.

"Smart people want more knowledge. But a foolish person just wants more foolishness."

—Who will end up happier in the long run, Conrad or Micah? Why?

—Why is gaining more knowledge important?

Further Reading: II Timothy 2:15

DAY 139

Proverbs 15:15 "Every day is hard for those who suffer. But a happy heart makes it like a continual feast."

A HAPPY HEART

Lisa had a very severe form of arthritis. It seemed as though all of her joints hurt continually. Sometimes the pain was so bad that she couldn't sleep at night.

You would think all this suffering would cause Lisa to be bitter, but actually she was a very encouraging person. When her friends went through difficult times, she always understood because she knew what it was like to be troubled. She would cheer them up and help them to understand that God loved them In spite of their difficulty. Lisa may have been handicapped on the outside, but she had great freedom inside. Few people ever experience the amount of joy she knew.

"Every day is hard for those who suffer. But a happy heart makes it like a continual feast."

—How is a happy heart like a continual feast?

—What difference will a happy heart make in our suffering?

Further Reading: Philippians 4:4, 7–8

DAY 140

Proverbs 15:16 "It is better to be poor and respect the Lord than to be wealthy and have much trouble."

WHICH IS BETTER?

David's parents didn't have much money. Sometimes at the end of the month, it seemed like all they had in the house to eat was peanut butter and oatmeal. But, they were great parents who loved David a lot. Their family spent a lot of time together. They had daily devotional time as a family and would often play games together or go hiking at a local forest preserve. It was a good family and David wouldn't trade it for the entire world.

Felix had a very wealthy father. His dad traveled all over the world with his business. He was rarely home. Because of all his travel, Felix's mother grew tired of being alone and filed for a divorce. Their family never did anything together, and although Felix had everything money could buy, he was a very unhappy boy.

"It is better to be poor and respect the Lord than to be wealthy and have much trouble."

—Why was David's situation better than Felix's life?

—Was it the money or their parents' attitude toward God that made the difference in their lives?

Further Reading: Psalm 37:16

DAY 141

Proverbs 15:22 "Plans fail without good advice. But plans succeed when you get advice from many others."

ADVICE

Beth thought that she was old enough to babysit. She had an older sister who babysat and Beth knew that she started watching other's children when she was Beth's age.

The trouble was that since Beth had never babysat before, she wasn't sure whether she would be good at it. She began to pray that God would give her wisdom concerning whether she should give several couples her name.

Beth also felt she couldn't make this decision alone. She decided to talk to her big sister who had a lot of experience babysitting. She also talked to her parents and a friend who had begun babysitting for a neighbor. Finally, she talked to several of the families in her church to find out what they wanted in a babysitter.

After all this counsel, Beth knew that she was ready to babysit and that she would do a good job. "Plans fail without good advice. But plans succeed when you get advice from others."

—How does advice help us in the decisions we make?

—How should we decide who to go to for advice?

Further Reading: Proverbs 13:10

DAY 142

Proverbs 15:27 "A greedy person brings trouble to his family. But the person who can't be paid to do wrong will live."

THE PROBLEM WITH GREED

Mr. Lisle was an inspector for the state. He went to factories and checked everything to make sure it was safe for the employees. At one particular factory the owner, Mr. Johnson, paid him to not report the things that were wrong. This saved the owner of the factory the money it would take to correct the safety hazards.

When Mr. Lisle was replaced by another inspector, Mr. Johnson asked him if he could be paid to overlook the problems. The new inspector was a Christian. He knew it would be wrong to take a bribe to cover up the safety problems. He also didn't want to be responsible for anyone getting hurt. Therefore he refused to take money from Mr. Johnson.

"A greedy person brings trouble to his family. But the person who can't be paid to do wrong will live."

—What is wrong with greed?

—Why must we be careful to never let someone pay us to do something wrong?

Further Reading: I Timothy 6:11

DAY 143

Proverbs 15:29 "The Lord does not listen to the wicked. But he hears the prayers of those who do right."

DO YOU KNOW GOD?

Anna noticed that Eliza was in the corner crying. She went over and sat beside her. "Can I help, Eliza?"

"No! No one can help. My parents hate each other, they hate me, and I hate everybody. Nobody can help me!"

"God can," Anna replied softly.

"Oh, sure. I keep praying for my parents but God never listens. They are still fighting."

"Do you know God, Eliza? You can't start asking Him for things until you know Him," Anna added gently.

"What do you mean 'know Him'? What are you talking about Anna?"

"If you've got some time, I'd like to explain it to you, Eliza. I know you don't feel anyone loves you, but God really does. In fact, I've been praying for you lately..."

Eliza was ready to listen.

—Why didn't Eliza feel like her prayers were being answered?

—How did Anna help her understand God better?

Further Reading: Psalm 145:18–19

DAY 144

Proverbs 15:33 "Respect for the Lord will teach you wisdom. If you want to be honored, you must not be proud."

GOD FIRST

John thought he knew everything. He was a smart kid and he let everyone know it as often as possible. Even in Sunday school class, he thought he knew all the answers. He did know things like "Where was Moses born?" or "Who was the left-handed judge?" but he didn't know the really important things.

John had no idea how to put God first in his life. He knew facts about God but he didn't really know God. He never read his Bible unless he had to. He never thought about God. He didn't even try to obey the things he knew. John knew a lot but he was not a wise person.

"Respect for the Lord will teach you wisdom. If you want to be honored, you must not be proud."

—What was wrong with John's knowledge?

—How can he learn wisdom?

Further Reading: Jeremiah 10:6–7

DAY 145

Proverbs 16:1–2 "People make plans in their hearts. But only the Lord can make those plans come true. A person may believe he is doing right. But the Lord will judge his reasons."

THE HEART IS WHAT COUNTS

Mrs. James was tired of being poor, so when she saw an advertisement for winning a free trip on a cruise liner, she decided that her family would be the winners. She filled out the form, sent it in, and began praying that she would win. She prayed so long and hard about it that she even began to pack to get ready for it.

On the day of the drawing, Mrs. James burst into tears. She couldn't believe it. She had not won. Later that day, although she was feeling depressed, she decided to read her Bible. She came across Proverbs 16:1-2, "People make plans in their hearts. But only the Lord can make those plans come true. A person may believe he is doing right. But the Lord will judge his reasons."

Mrs. James realized that when she prayed, she only cared about getting what she wanted. She had not been interested in God's will for her family, nor had she been content in the things God had already given her.

—What was wrong with Mrs. James' prayer?

—What would have been a better prayer?

Further Reading: Proverbs 16:3–4

DAY 146

Proverbs16:6 "Love and truth bring forgiveness of sin. By respecting the Lord you will avoid evil."

FORGIVENESS

Lena grew up in a home that did not honor God. In fact, she knew nothing about God. When Jean invited her to church, Lena agreed out of curiosity. Everything went well until the prayer time. Lena kept nudging Jean, asking her when it was going to be over. "What are we doing, anyway?" she whispered.

All of a sudden, Jean understood why Lena did so many things that were wrong. Since Lena didn't know God, she had no idea how to please Him. Lena began coming to church with Jean regularly. Gradually she came to understand that Jesus Christ wanted to forgive her sin and make her into a person who would love and obey Him. She began to have a great respect for God so that she wanted good things for her life rather than evil things.

"Love and truth bring forgiveness of sin. By respecting the Lord you will avoid evil."

—How did love and truth bring Lena to Jesus Christ?

—How did her new respect for the Lord change her life?

Further Reading: 2 Corinthians 5:17

DAY 147

Proverbs16:12 "Kings hate those who do wrong because governments only last if they are fair."

A FAIR GOVERNMENT

Years ago the communist world in Europe seemed immovable. No one could imagine that the Eastern Bloc countries would ever change. Now they have crumbled like an old brick.

The reason for this change is that the people within these systems knew that it was an unfair way to rule. Under communism, their basic freedoms were violated. Christians and Jews particularly suffered under the communist regimes because of their firm refusal to give up their faith.

The same has been true through the centuries of governments that treat their citizens unfairly. Eventually people rebel under a system that abuses their rights and the country is taken over by another group.

"Kings hate those who do wrong because governments only last if they are fair."

—Why will a government not last unless it is fair?

—How does wrong-doing make a government become unfair?

—What are some injustices in our own country?

Further Reading: Romans 13:1

DAY 148

Proverbs 16:16 "It is better to get wisdom than gold. It is better to choose understanding than silver!"

GOLD AND SILVER

Matt and Rory both entered college at the same time but each of them had very different goals. Rory wanted to be successful. He majored in business administration and began his own business while in school. His ambition was to become a millionaire by the time he was thirty years old.

Matt had a much different view of college than Rory. He majored in education because he wanted to help others learn. He spent most of his spare time working for volunteer organizations so that he could learn to understand people better. Matt also was a student of the Bible. He knew if he didn't understand God that he would have nothing to offer other people.

"It is better to get wisdom than gold. It is better to choose understanding than silver!"

—Why is wisdom better than gold and understanding better than silver?

—How do we gain wisdom and understanding?

Further Reading: Proverbs 8:10–19

DAY 149

Proverbs 16:17 "A good person stays away from evil. A person who watches what he does protects his life."

WATCH WHAT YOU DO

Frank had a group of friends in grade school who were a lot of fun. But as he grew older, he noticed that some of the boys he spent time with began doing things that were wrong.

"Hey Frank, do you want to go with us to Jerry's house? His parents aren't home so we've invited some girls over there too. We're going to listen to some music and Doug's bringing an X-rated video of his dad's. It should be exciting! You aren't going to chicken out on us, are you?"

Frank shuddered as he thought how he, Jerry, and Doug used to play baseball as entertainment. He knew the time had come to part ways with his boyhood friends.

"A good person stays away from evil. A person who watches what he does protects his life."

—Why does a good person need to stay away from evil?

—How do we protect our life by staying away from evil?

Further Reading: Isaiah 35:8

DAY 150

Proverbs 16:20 "Whoever pays attention to what he is taught will succeed. And whoever trusts the Lord will be happy."

LOVE TO LEARN

Charity loved to learn. She listened carefully during devotional time with her family, paid attention during Sunday school, and worked hard at school.

Her genuine desire to learn made all of these things easier, even enjoyable. Because of this, Charity found her decisions were fairly easy to make. When she entered college, she knew that she wanted to serve God with her life. As she dated men, she knew that she would only be happy with a man who loved God. Her life was balanced, orderly, and fulfilling. The decisions she made fit into the purposes for which God made her.

"Whoever pays attention to what he is taught will succeed. And whoever trusts the Lord will be happy." The way we live now will affect the people we will become.

—Why was Charity's life successful?

—How did her trust in the Lord make her happy?

Further Reading: Jeremiah 17:7–8

DAY 151

Proverbs 16:21 "A wise person is known for his understanding. He wins people to his side with pleasant words."

PLEASANT WORDS

"What do you think you are doing?" Jeremy yelled as he walked into the room. "You have no business being in my room!"

His little sister, Colleen, burst into tears as her big brother screamed at her.

Their oldest sister heard the conversation and understood what was going on. Her brother wanted his room to be private and his little sister was curious as to what was in his mysterious room. She decided to be the peacemaker.

"Jeremy, you scared her. I know you don't want her in your room, but there's a better way to tell her.

"Colleen, this is Jeremy's room. I'll give you a tour so that you can see what is here. But you must be careful not to touch his things, O.K.?"

Jeremy looked at his little sister as she dried her eyes.

"That's alright, Sis. I'll give Colleen the tour. Take my hand, Colleen?" he asked gently.

—What was wrong with Jeremy's words at the beginning of our story?

—Why do pleasant words do so much more good than angry ones?

Further Reading: Hosea 14:9

DAY 152

Proverbs 16:23 "A wise person's mind tells him what to say. This helps him to teach others better."

THINK BEFORE YOU SPEAK

Dan was a thoughtful person. Everyone who knew him respected him. They knew that what he had to say was worthwhile. As a result, whenever they had a problem they would come to Dan for advice. He always counseled them wisely, being careful to pray for wisdom and to stick to the instruction he had learned in God's Word. The words that came out of his mouth were a result of the good things Jesus Christ had done in his life.

"A wise person's mind tells him what to say. This helps him to teach others better." We need to be training our minds to think correctly. God would like to use us all to teach others in His way. Only as we learn His way ourselves will we be able to do this.

—Why do we need to be wise before we can teach others?

—Where do we find such wisdom?

Further Reading: Psalm 37:30–31

DAY 153

Proverbs 16:26 "The worker's hunger helps him. His desire to eat makes him work."

GOOD HUNGER

Hal took a paper route this year. It was his first real job. Every morning he had to get up at six o'clock so that he could deliver his papers before school. After a few months of this, he was really tired of it. He complained so much that his mother asked him why he didn't just quit.

"I've never had any money to spend, Mom. Now I do, so it's worth all the hassle. I'll try not to complain so much."

So Hal has kept his paper route and is learning to be responsible and dedicated through it. And besides, he has spending money.

"The worker's hunger helps him. His desire to eat makes him work."

—Why is work so good for us?

—How does our hunger or our desire to make our life better make us work harder?

Further Reading: Ecclesiastes 5:12

DAY 154

Proverbs 16:28 "An evil person causes trouble. And a person who gossips ruins friendships."

GOSSIP

"Did you hear about Chloe?" whispered Andrea. "I heard that her parents are going to get a divorce."

"Really?" asked Ella. "I thought her parents were getting counseling."

"That's not what Ed told me. He heard that Chloe is afraid to go home anymore."

"I wonder who started all these rumors about Chloe." Marcy said. "I know for a fact that none of them are true. Chloe has wonderful parents. They did get some counseling so that they could work through a few problems but it really helped. They have one of the best marriages I know. So you all can stop this gossip right now!"

Marcy's eyes snapped like they always did when she meant something and so the girls said no more about Chloe's parents.

"An evil person causes trouble. And a person who gossips ruins friendships."

—What kind of damage could the gossip in this story have done?

—How might it have ruined the girls' friendship with Chloe?

Further Reading: Proverbs 16:28–30

DAY 155

Proverbs 16:31 "Gray hair is like a crown of honor. You earn it by living a good life."

THE CROWN OF GRAY HAIR

"I'm going to go see Mr. Kirkman. Do you want to go with me?" Mark asked Rob.

"That old man? What in the world do you talk to him about?"

"Lots of things. He's really smart. He has been all over the world in the service. I learn a lot from him."

"I don't get it — spending time with some old person."

"I figure he knows a lot more than I do. I hope I end up as interesting as he is."

"I hope I never get that old."

"What are you talking about? It would be great to be old enough to really know what life is all about. Mr. Kirkman helps me understand God a lot better. Just come with me this once."

Mark knew that "Gray hair is like a crown of honor. You earn it by living a good life."

—Why is it an honor to have lived to an old age?

—How does the way you live determine what kind of person you will be when you are old?

Further Reading: Job 12:12

DAY 156

Proverbs 16:32 "Patience is better than strength. Controlling your temper is better than capturing a city."

TRUE STRENGTH

"Alright, Ralph. What do you think you are doing at our table?" Sam boomed as several other big boys crowded around the table, looking as threatening as possible. "Unless you move right now, I'll have to teach you a lesson."

"I didn't know it was your table," Ralph replied calmly but firmly. "I'll be done eating in a minute, and then it will be all yours."

"Not good enough, Pickle Brain. Move it now!" Sam yelled.

"I don't want a quarrel with you, Sam. You know you could beat me up if you wanted to but it's not right for you to make me move. By the time you get through the line, I'll be done. The table will be all yours."

Sam scowled at Ralph but let it go. He and the other boys rumbled off muttering threats under their breath.

"Patience is better than strength. Controlling your temper is better than capturing a city."

—Which boy do you think really had the most strength—Sam with his muscles or Ralph with his firm, quiet character?

—Which do you think will be more successful in life?

Further Reading: Proverbs 15:1

DAY 157

Proverbs 17:1 "It is better to eat a dry crust of bread in peace than to have a feast where there is quarreling."

PEACE OR QUARRELING

Carla's family lived a very simple life. They had everything they needed but not a lot of extras. Her parents were loving, kind people who always tried to do what was right. It was always a pleasure to be in Carla's home because they always welcomed you as one of the family. All who entered their house felt that it was a peaceful, comfortable place to be.

Elaine had a very different situation. Her parents were so busy that they hardly ever saw each other. Actually, Elaine thought that was good because when they were together, they fought continually. They went out to eat almost every night, which kept them from fighting since they were In publlc. It also kept them from talking to each other. Elaine wished her family could be more like Carla's.

"It is better to eat a dry crust of bread in peace than to have a feast where there is quarreling."

—Why is peace more important than riches in a home?

—How do you feel when everyone is quarreling?

—What can we do to avoid quarrels?

Further Reading: Titus 3:10–11

DAY 158

Proverbs 17:2 "A wise servant will rule over his master's disgraceful son. And he will even inherit a share of what the master leaves his sons."

A WISE SERVANT AND A DISGRACEFUL SON

Mr. Kelley worked hard at his business. He built it up from small beginnings in his basement to a very successful company. From the start, he hired Mr. Richmond to help him in his business. Mr. Richmond was a diligent worker and respected Mr. Kelley. He was proud to work for him, always trying to do his best.

When Mr. Kelley's son, Wyatt, became old enough to help with the business, he offered him a job. Wyatt only did what he absolutely had to. He showed no respect for his father and no love for the company. He often missed days of work, expecting his father to excuse him. As Mr. Kelley grew old, he decided to leave his business to Mr. Richmond rather than his son.

"A wise servant will rule over his master's disgraceful son. And he will even inherit a share of what the master leaves his sons."

—How was Wyatt a disgraceful son in our story?

—How was Mr. Richmond wise?

Further Reading: Colossians 3:17

DAY 159

Proverbs 17:3 "A hot furnace tests silver and gold. In the same way, the Lord tests a person's heart."

A HOT FURNACE

Mont grew up in a loving home. His parents always expected a lot from him and he learned to be disciplined. They taught him that loving God was more important than anything else in the world. Mont also learned that God loved him more than he could imagine.

When he was sixteen years old, he was in a terrible automobile accident. Mont broke both of his legs and cracked a few ribs. As a result, he spent many months in the hospital. During that time, he remembered all his parents had taught him about God. Although he often asked God why the accident had to happen, he never turned away from God or felt that God didn't love him. In fact, he feels the experience drew him much closer to God.

Mont was tested in a hot furnace and proved himself true.

—How are hard things like being put in a hot furnace?

—How does God use hard things to test our hearts?

Further Reading: I Chronicles 29:17

DAY 160

Proverbs 17:5 "If you make fun of the poor, you insult God, who made them. If you laugh at someone's trouble, you will be punished."

NEVER LAUGH AT ANOTHER'S TROUBLE

"Guess what I found out," Lucy asked with a wicked grin on her face.

Jeanette just looked back at her without answering.

Lucy continued, "Nina is going to fail this year. I think it serves her right and I'm going to make sure everyone knows about it."

"Don't you dare, Lucy!" Jeanette answered sternly. "Poor Nina. Her dad lost his job this year and her mother has been working double-time to make ends meet. It has been a terrible year for her. No wonder she has had trouble in school."

Lucy threw her head back and laughed. "Big deal. I've got juicy news and I'm not keeping it to myself."

Jeanette shook her head as she looked at Lucy. "Someday it will be you who is in trouble, Lucy, and no one is going to care."

"If you make fun of the poor, you insult God, who made them. If you laugh at someone's trouble, you will be punished."

—Why do we insult God if we make fun of the poor?

—Why is it wrong to laugh at other's trouble?

—What should Lucy have done?

Further Reading: Obadiah 12

DAY 161

Proverbs 17:6 "Grandchildren are the reward of old people. And children are proud of their parents."

THE REWARD

It was a big day at church for the Lyman family. Owen was going to be baptized and so both sets of grandparents were coming into town to be there. Owen felt so pleased when his grandparents walked through the door and greeted him with a big hug. One part of him told him that he was too old for this kind of attention from his grandparents. The other part of him told him he would never be too old to enjoy this.

The day was going to be special for another reason too. Owen's dad was going to get up before the entire church to share with them how Jesus Christ had changed his life. As his dad walked up to the front of the church, Owen felt prouder of his father than at any other time of his life. He thought it took a lot of guts to stand for Christ like that. Owen wanted to be just like his dad.

"Grandchildren are the reward of old people. And children are proud of their parents."

—How are grandchildren a reward to old people?

—What makes children proud of their parents?

Further Reading: Genesis 48:15–16

DAY 162

Proverbs 17:13 "If a person gives evil in return for good, his house will always be full of trouble."

A HOUSE OF TROUBLE

Janet was excited. She had worked on a picture all day to give her brother for his birthday. She put all sorts of things in it that she thought he liked. She had to admit that it turned out very well. Janet imagined how pleased he would be when she gave it to him.

When he got home from his friend's house she yelled, "Happy Birthday!" and handed him the picture.

"What's this?" he asked as he looked at the picture. "You call this art? Is that supposed to be a tree? You'd better take lessons, Janet." He then wadded the paper up and threw it on the couch.

Janet went over to pick up the paper. She ran to her room and tore the picture into many pieces. As she threw it away, the tears welled in her eyes. "I'll never do anything for him again," she said with determination.

"If a person gives evil in return for good, his house will always be full of trouble."

—How did Janet's brother start trouble in the house?

—What does it do to the other person when we don't notice the good they do?

Further Reading: Psalm 35:12

DAY 163

Proverbs 17:17 "A friend loves you all the time. A brother is always there to help you."

A FRIEND AND BROTHER

Luke walked into the house with a sad face.

"What's wrong with you?" Justin, his twin brother, asked.

"I've got a book report due tomorrow but I forgot to bring the book home."

"Uh-oh, that is bad news. Tell you what, I heard Jon say that he was reading the same book you were. Let's walk over there now and see if we can borrow it. If that doesn't work, we can always try the library."

Luke looked at Justin with admiration and relief. "Thanks, Justin. That's what I needed — someone to get me going in the right direction. You are a great brother."

"I know," Justin smiled broadly.

"A friend loves you all the time. A brother is always there to help you."

—Is somebody really a friend if they don't help you when you need it?

—Can a brother be a friend too?

—Who is the one friend we can always count on?

Further Reading: John 15:12–17

DAY 164

Proverbs 17:19 "Whoever loves to quarrel loves to sin. Whoever is proud is asking for trouble."

THE SIN OF QUARRELING

The gospel singing group met in the Jamison's basement to practice for an upcoming concert. They invited friends and neighbors to come listen if they wanted to. One neighbor who came was the kind of person who just loved to cause trouble.

Right away he said to Mr. Jamison, "You know, I really can't stand gospel music. I think I'll just flip the radio on." He then turned the radio on as loud as he could. Mr. Jamison turned it off and moved the radio to another room.

Next, the neighbor went to Mrs. Jamison and complained about her housekeeping. "Did you see all the dust on that table? I'm surprised you let anyone in here." Mrs. Jamison handed him a dust rag.

"Whoever loves to quarrel loves to sin. Whoever is proud is asking for trouble." The Jamisons understood that this man loved to quarrel. They were careful that he didn't cause them to sin.

—Why is loving to quarrel a sin?

—What did the Jamisons do that was right?

Further Reading: Proverbs 17:20–21, 27–28

DAY 165

Proverbs 17:22 "A happy heart is like good medicine. But a broken spirit drains your strength."

GOOD MEDICINE

Lori was very sick. She was hospitalized for the second time with cancer. This was perhaps the hardest time because she had licked cancer once but now it was back again.

Her friends knew that her spirit was especially low. They could see her getting weaker every day, so they devised a plan. Each day one of them would go in to her room, read Scripture, tell jokes, pray with her, and just talk.

After a few weeks of this, they saw Lori's spirits rise. She began to talk about getting rid of her cancer once and for all. She was even able to make jokes about losing her hair.

Lori's friends knew that "A happy heart is like good medicine. But a broken spirit drains your strength."

—How was Lori's broken spirit draining her strength?

—How did Lori's friends provide "good medicine" for her?

Further Reading: II Corinthians 10:3–5

DAY 166

Proverbs 17:26 "It is not good to punish those who have done what is right. Nor is it good to punish leaders for being honest."

IT IS NOT GOOD

There have been times in our country, as in all countries, where the good are punished. When the African-American people began to speak up for their rights, many of them were arrested and sent to jail. The improvements that the blacks in our country have experienced are due to these brave men and women who did what was right in spite of punishment.

Many today are suffering fines and jail sentences for their stand against social injustices. They too are willing to be punished because they believe that a great wrong is being done.

We need to pray for our country's leaders to be able to recognize right from wrong and protect the good.

—Why do we need to pray for the leaders of our country? Let's do so right now.

Further Reading: Proverbs 17:23–24

DAY 167

Proverbs 18:1 "An unfriendly person cares only about himself. He makes fun of all wisdom."

THE UNFRIENDLY

Duane was fifteen and had been feeling as though he was on top of the world. He was included in the "in" group at school and worked hard at doing all the things they would want him to do.

During a school play Esther, who went to Duane's church, saw him with his friends. Esther was seven years old and was delighted to see a familiar face. She ran up to Duane in front of his friends. "Hi, Duane!" she called. "Remember me?"

"Yeah, get out of here, kid," he replied as he and his friends had a good laugh at her expense.

Esther turned away, heartbroken at Duane's response. She felt the people at church were special but Duane obviously didn't care about her.

"An unfriendly person cares only about himself. He makes fun of all wisdom."

—How did Duane show that he cared only about himself?

—What would have been a better way for him to respond to Esther?

Further Reading: Colossians 3:12

DAY 168

Proverbs 18:6 "A fool's words start quarrels. They make people want to give him a beating."

FOOLISH WORDS

Eric was always bragging. "I can beat up anybody here," is how he usually began his conversations. "What are you looking at me that way for?" was another one of his favorite lines. "You trying to start trouble?" could be heard from him daily.

Eric could manage to make everyone mad at him within a few minutes. The response he got from others was consistent. If they were foolish, they would take his challenge and pick a fight with him. If they were wise, they would ignore him. But, it was true that they all felt like beating Eric up at one time or another.

"A fool's words start quarrels. They make people want to give him a beating."

—How did Eric's words make people mad at him?

—What could someone have done to help Eric change?

Further Reading: Proverbs 18:7–8

DAY 169

Proverbs 18:9 "A person who doesn't work hard is just like a person who destroys things."

THE DESTROYER

Amanda hated her after-school job. She had only been working at a fast-food restaurant for a week but she already detested it. The only reason she went at all was that she wanted the money.

When her supervisor was around, she pretended to work very hard but when he wasn't looking, she would continually find ways to get out of her work. She visited the restroom often or would wash the same table over three times while she talked to a friend.

One day a fellow worker of Amanda's became angry with her. "You might as well add more hours on to our work schedule, Amanda. We all have to do your work for you! Don't you see you are stealing the restaurant's money by not working for it?

Amanda just turned up her nose and visited the restroom again.

—How was Amanda's laziness making it hard for everyone else?

—Was she earning her money or stealing it?

Further Reading: Philippians 2:13

DAY 170

Proverbs 18:10 "The Lord is like a strong tower. Those who do what is right can run to him for safety."

A STRONG TOWER

Every day at school, Rory had to face the same thing. Oscar Kline, the bully, tormented everyone daily. Now Rory was not a big kid; he was much smaller than Oscar and he grew more frightened of him each day. Oscar always sounded so threatening, leaving little doubt that he would just love to cause you harm.

At school Oscar couldn't do much, but after school he really terrified Rory on the walk home. One day Oscar began to pick on Tim, who was a very shy boy. He boxed him around and made fun of his shyness. Finally, Oscar pushed Tim into a mud puddle, sticking his face in it. Something inside of Rory was screaming. He could take no more. He prayed for strength and then, shoving everyone aside, he pushed Oscar off of Tim and helped Tim up. He stood defiantly staring at Oscar. Then to Rory's surprise, one boy after another came to stand by him in his rebellion against Oscar. Oscar turned with a scowl and headed home.

"The Lord is like a strong tower. Those who do what is right can run to him for safety."

—How was the Lord like a strong tower to Rory?

—How can he be a strong tower for you?

Further Reading: 2 Samuel 22:2–3

DAY 171

Proverbs 18:17 "The first person to tell his side of a story seems right. But that may change when somebody comes and asks him questions."

TWO SIDES TO A STORY

Mom heard Bev and Amy at it again. From the bedroom which they shared, she could hear their voices raised in anger. Soon Amy came stomping out, slamming the door behind her.

"Mom, I can't take her anymore. Do you know what she did now? She broke the new figurine Grandma gave me. It was special to me and she did it just to make me mad. How can she be so mean?" Amy was now crying and obviously upset.

Mom felt angry at Bev. It did seem that she often tried to make Amy mad but this was the last straw. She went into their room and challenged Bev.

"Why did you break your sister's figurine? I can't believe you would do that."

Bev looked up at her mom with tears rolling down her face. "I feel awful, Mom. Amy wouldn't let me finish telling her. I know I've been mean to her lately so I thought I would surprise her by cleaning up our room. When I was rearranging the dresser, the figurine broke. I'm so sorry."

Mother took Bev in her arms and called Amy into the room.

—Why should we always be careful to hear the other person's side of a story?

—How would this story have been different if Amy had listened to Bev?

Further Reading: Proverbs 18:15–19

DAY 172

Proverbs 18:24 "Some friends may ruin you. But a real friend will be more loyal than a brother."

A REAL FRIEND

Lyle was a popular person. Everyone liked him at school. He could always say a funny thing at just the right time and he knew how to act in any group that he was in.

The group at school he most enjoyed was a fun-loving party bunch. They had the best parties, clothes, cars, and houses. The trouble was that Lyle was a Christian but nobody else in this group was. As a result, they wanted to do things he felt very uncomfortable with. They listened to heavy metal rock music that was definitely not Christian, experimented with sex and alcohol, and talked about trying some new drug.

Lyle wanted to be part of this group so badly that he tried to ignore the things they were doing while still being a part of the group. But, Lyle found this harder and harder to do. It was just easier to give in and try the stuff they were doing.

Fortunately, Lyle had a good friend who was also a Christian. This friend loyally warned Lyle of the wrongs this group was leading him into. At last, Lyle left the group.

"Some friends may ruin you. But a real friend will be more loyal than a brother."

—How can friends ruin us?

—What should we look for in a friend?

Further Reading: Proverbs 18:20–24

DAY 173

Proverbs 19:2 "Enthusiasm without knowledge is not good. If you act too quickly, you might make a mistake."

PATIENCE

Georgia burst through the door yelling excitedly, "Mom, guess what! Mina can order me a china doll for just $5! Remember those beautiful dolls we saw last summer? They cost about $80. Mina can get me one for $5. I'm going to give her my money now."

"Have you seen one of these dolls, Georgia?" her mother asked.

"No, but it's such a good deal. I've always wanted a china doll."

"I'd find out more about it first, Georgia."

"She's got to have the money tonight to place the order, Mom. I'll be back in a few minutes after I take the money to Mina."

A few weeks later Georgia received her $5 doll. It was only six inches tall and about as homely as a doll can be. She wished she had taken her time before ordering it.

"Enthusiasm without knowledge is not good. If you act too quickly, you might make a mistake."

—Why should we take our time before making a decision?

—What else should we do besides taking our time as we make a decision?

Further Reading: Proverbs 21:5

DAY 174

Proverbs 19:3 "A person's own foolishness ruins his life. But in his mind he blames the Lord for it."

A FOOLISH MAN

Mr. Oswald was a terrible decision maker. Rather than praying about what God wanted him to do, he just did what he felt like doing. As a result, he decided to start his own business. At first the business went very well, but after about a year he began to lose customers. By the time another year had passed, his business folded.

Rather than learning from his mistake, Mr. Oswald blamed God for his lack of success. He felt that God let him down and he began to become bitter towards the Lord. He quit going to church and pulled away from his Christian friends.

If Mr. Oswald had been honest, he would have realized that he brought his trouble upon himself.

"A person's own foolishness ruins his life. But in his mind he blames the Lord for it."

—How did Mr. Oswald's foolishness ruin his life?

—Why did he blame the Lord for it?

Further Reading: Proverbs 11:3

DAY 175

Proverbs 19:14 "Houses and wealth are inherited from parents. But a wise wife is a gift from the Lord."

A GIFT FROM GOD

Every time Marshall turned on the television, he saw a beautiful girl advertising something. He decided that when he married, it would be to the prettiest girl around.

He noticed that his neighbor, Mrs. Trent, was a beautiful woman. "Just the kind of woman I'd like to marry someday" he thought. However, later that day he heard a conversation between his parents.

"We need to pray for the Trents, Dear," his mother said. "She told me today that they are seriously in debt because of all the money she spent on clothes. You know, she is a very unhappy woman. I rarely see her smile about anything these days. I think they have real trouble. She has such a cold heart."

Marshall began to think differently about what would make a good wife. Maybe all the commercials were wrong.

"Houses and wealth are inherited from parents. But a wise wife is a gift from the Lord."

—What should a woman try to be according to this verse?

—What should a man look for in a wife?

—Why is being wise so important for a wife?

Further Reading: Proverbs 19:8

DAY 176

Proverbs 19:18 "Correct your son while there is still hope. Do not help him destroy himself."

CORRECT YOUR SON

The Johnsons lived next to a four-year-old boy named Leo. Leo loved to visit the Johnsons because they had a boy his age. These visits usually went well unless Leo couldn't have a toy he wanted. One day, he threw a fit over a toy his friend wouldn't give him. Leo became so angry that he broke his friend's toy in two rather than give it back. At this point Mrs. Johnson made Leo go home.

He went home in tears and his mother called Mrs. Johnson, angry with her. Even after Mrs. Johnson told her what happened, she stuck up for her son.

Sadly, Leo's mother was helping him to destroy himself. Even though she thought she loved him a great deal, she was teaching him that he could always have his way. He would grow up to be a selfish, disagreeable individual.

"Correct your son while there is still hope. Do not help him destroy himself."

—Why do we all need to be corrected?

—How will it destroy us if we are not corrected?

Further Reading: Proverbs 13:24; 19:20

DAY 177

Proverbs 19:23 "Those who respect the Lord will live and be content, unbothered by trouble."

THE BEST KIND OF LIFE

Ross was the kind of guy everyone respected. He made it very clear that he was a Christian and he lived a life that backed it up. No one made fun of his faith because they knew that he treated them well because of what he believed.

That's why everyone was surprised when Ross found out that he had a bad heart. Even at his young age, he would have to undergo open-heart surgery. Many of his friends expected to see Ross' faith crumble, but instead they saw it strengthen. Ross knew that God made him, knew him, and loved him. He also knew that nothing could ever change those three facts. Even in the midst of the frightening surgery he had to face (and he was frightened), he was deeply content.

"Those who respect the Lord will live and be content, unbothered by trouble."

—How does respect for the Lord cause us to be content?

—How does respect for the Lord cause us to be unbothered by trouble?

Further Reading: I Samuel 12:24

DAY 178

Proverbs 20:1 "Wine and beer make people loud and uncontrolled. It is not wise to get drunk on them."

LOUD AND UNCONTROLLED

Malcolm and his friends had attended the same church for many years. They knew that the Bible had strong warnings against getting drunk. But one Saturday night, a few of their other friends invited them over to try some beer. They just wanted to know what it was like to get drunk, so they went.

Because they weren't used to drinking alcohol, they became drunk very quickly. Malcolm remembered laughing and crying a lot but he also knew he was too drunk to get home by himself. He finally had to call his parents to come get him.

Besides facing their anger and being grounded, Malcolm spent a miserable night. It was worse than the flu. He vomited repeatedly and had the worst headache of his life. The next time someone suggested to Malcolm that he get drunk, he didn't even have to think before answering, "No!"

—Why is it unwise to get drunk?

—What can you say to a friend who wants you to get drunk with him or her?

Further Reading: Romans 13:13–14

DAY 179

Proverbs 20:5 "Understanding a person's thoughts is as hard as getting water from a deep well. But someone with understanding can find the wisdom there."

WATER FROM A DEEP WELL

"I don't understand that brother of mine," yelled Erin as she walked into the kitchen. "He just told me I couldn't even look at his stamp collection and then he gave it to Martin to take home overnight. Does that make sense to you?"

Erin's mother sighed and decided to find out what her son was thinking. "What's going on with the stamps?" she asked him.

"I just don't want Erin looking at them!" he yelled.

"Can you tell me why?" his mother asked softly.

"She never lets me see anything of hers!"

"Is that all?"

"I always have to share everything with her, Mom." He lowered his voice to a gentle tone. "I just need one thing that is all my own."

Mom nodded her head. She understood and decided to help Erin understand.

—Why is it important for us to ask questions when we don't understand someone?

—How does the way we ask questions determine what kind of answer we get?

Further Reading: Ephesians 4:1–3

DAY 180

Proverbs 20:9 "No one can say, 'I am innocent. I have never done anything wrong.'"

NO ONE IS INNOCENT

"I'm sure glad I'm not like that stuck-up Edna next door," Vivian exclaimed as she slammed the front door. "I waved to her and she never paid any attention to me. She thinks she's too good for the rest of us. I would never act like that to anyone."

"Well, Vivian," her mother replied gently, "I seem to remember a time last week when you wouldn't let your sister even come into your room to say hi to the friend you had over. Was that so different?"

"Of course it's different. She's a pest."

"Your sister doesn't see it as any different. She was just as hurt by your action as you were by Edna's."

"I don't care! It's just not the same!"

Proverbs 20:9 says, "No one can ever say, 'I am innocent. I have never done anything wrong.'" If we are honest with ourselves we will realize that we are no better than the next person is. We all need a savior to deliver us from our sins. Have you accepted Jesus Christ's forgiveness for your sins?

—Why are none of us innocent?

—How can we get rid of our sin?

Further Reading: I John 1:8–10

DAY 181

Proverbs 20:17 "When a person gets food dishonestly, it may taste sweet at first. But later he will feel as if he has a mouth full of gravel."

A MOUTH FULL OF GRAVEL

Derek noticed the music CD at his friend's house right away. It was a recording of his favorite singing group. He had tried to buy the same CD but all the stores had sold out of it. So while his friend was busy doing something else, Derek slipped the CD into his pocket.

As soon as he got home, he played it. He had wanted that CD so badly. Now he finally had it. Listening to it the first time, he felt enthusiastic about having it. But as he listened to it the second time, he began to feel awful. Derek knew that what he had done was wrong. In fact, it began to bother his conscience so much that he couldn't even enjoy listening to it anymore. He decided to return it to his friend.

"When a person gets food dishonestly, it may taste sweet at first. But later he will feel as if he has a mouth full of gravel."

—Why do we end up unhappy if we are dishonest?

—How can we avoid doing anything which is dishonest?

Further Reading: Ephesians 4:28

DAY 182

Proverbs 20:22 "Don't say, 'I'll pay you back for the evil you did.' Wait for the Lord. He will make things right."

THE LORD WILL MAKE THINGS RIGHT

"I hate that Desiree! She is the meanest person alive," Elise cried to her big sister. "Do you know what she did to me?"

"It must have been pretty bad from the look on your face," her sister replied.

"The worst! She told all the other girls that I was going to have a party without inviting any of them. Now they are all mad at me. No one would even talk to me today."

"Is it true? Are you having a party?"

"Of course not. That's just what I mean. Desiree is hateful. But I'm going to get her back. On my birthday I'm going to invite everyone but her. I'll make sure she knows it too. In fact, I'll make sure the whole school knows it! Boy, will she be humiliated."

"I wouldn't do that, Elise. Then you will be no better than she is. Jesus says we are to return love for hatred."

"That's impossible. What does He know about something like this?"

"Think about it, Elise. I think He knows a lot about it. What He went through was a lot worse than what you are facing."

—What was wrong with Elise's attitude?

—What should have been her attitude?

Further Reading: Matthew 5:38–39

DAY 183

Proverbs 21:2 "A person may believe he is doing right. But the Lord judges his reasons."

WHAT ARE YOUR REASONS?

Eric had trouble making friends. He was big and loud which caused him to overwhelm people. But he finally found a friend in Jonah. Jonah didn't seem to mind any of Eric's faults. He was a true friend.

The trouble was that Eric was always afraid of losing Jonah as a friend. He couldn't believe that Jonah would stick by him. So Eric began to shower Jonah with presents. He bought him things all the time to insure that Jonah would remain his friend.

Eric's mother thought that he was just being kind to his friend. She saw his generosity as a good thing. But Eric's father was worried about the reason behind all the gift giving. In talking to Eric, he discovered that Eric was trying to buy his friend's loyalty. His father helped him to see that if a friend will not remain true to you without being bought, he is no friend at all. Eric's actions were good but his reasons were poor.

"A person may believe he is doing right. But the Lord judges his reasons."

—What was wrong with what Eric was doing?

—How can our actions seem right while our reasons are wrong?

Further Reading: Proverbs 16:2

DAY 184

Proverbs 21:11 "Punish a person who makes fun of wisdom, and he will become wise. But just teach a wise person, and he will get knowledge."

WISDOM WITHOUT PUNISHMENT

"I don't have to do what you say," yelled Megan. "You're not my mother!"

"But you are in my house, Megan. While you are here, you must obey our rules," Mrs. Knutson replied.

"Well, I don't see what's wrong with sliding down a railing. You're just mean."

"You don't have to understand my reasons but you do have to obey me. Now, I would like you to go home because of the way you acted. If you can live by our rules, you are welcome back. If not, you may not come here."

Megan left in a burst of tears because she didn't get her way, but the next time she came she behaved better. Megan was a person who made fun of wisdom. She had to be punished before she could be taught.

Pray that you will be a wise person who can be taught without having to be punished first.

—Why did Megan have so much trouble following the rules?

—What needed to change in her heart?

Further Reading: Proverbs 19:25

DAY 185

Proverbs 21:13 "If you ignore the poor when they cry for help, you also will cry for help and not be answered."

CRY FOR HELP

"That neighbor kid came over again to ask if he could borrow some more groceries," Terry said to his friend, Mike.

"That's the family whose dad left them, isn't it?"

"Yeah. I can't stand that family. They are leeches."

"I don't know, Terry. They are trying to do the right thing. It's really tough for their mom to make ends meet since their dad left. If we can help them a little with groceries, I'm all for it."

"You sap, Mike. Anybody could take you in. All I know is that I'll never ask another person for help, no matter what."

"It could be no one would help you if you asked, Terry. Especially if they have the same attitude you do right now."

Mike knew that "If you ignore the poor when they cry for help, you also will cry for help and not be answered." We never know when we may be the one in need.

—Why should we help the poor?

—What should be our attitude when we are helping others less fortunate than ourselves?

Further Reading: I John 3:17–18

DAY 186

Proverbs 21:15 "When things are done fairly, good people are happy, but evil people are frightened."

FAIRNESS

"Did you hear about the new teacher we are getting for science?" Mary whispered to Tony with a groan.

"Yeah, I hear he is really tough. I guess this is going to be the end of our straight-A record. It was easy to cheat with Mrs. Virgil as our teacher, but when this new guy comes, it's going to be all over," Tony answered sadly.

Meanwhile at the other end of the classroom, Nicole was talking to Julia.

"We are finally getting a new teacher. Maybe we will have a chance at a fair grade now. With the group in our class who always cheated, we never could get as good of grades as they did."

"I know," replied Julia. "Mrs. Virgil would never try to do anything to stop them. I'm so glad things are going to be fair now."

Mary, Tony, Nicole, and Julia were proving the truth of our proverb today. "When things are done fairly, good people are happy, but evil people are frightened."

—Why do evil people fear justice?

—Why are good people happy when things are done fairly?

Further Reading: Deuteronomy 32:4

DAY 187

Proverbs 21:17 "Whoever loves pleasure will become poor. Whoever loves wine and rich food will never be wealthy."

THE PROBLEM WITH PLEASURE

Don loved having fun. When he took his first job one winter shoveling the neighbor's walks, he made quite a bit of money. Money meant fun to Don so he would spend every last cent on junk food, video games, movies, and toys. He never learned to save money more than a week's time.

This concerned his parents because they knew that when Don was older that he would have to learn to save and to spend his money on necessities. He would never be able to buy a house, or a car, or any other large purchase unless he learned how to save. Don needed to see that money was not only to be spent on pleasure.

Therefore, they asked him to give away one tenth of his money earned to the church and to save another tenth of his money. They also refused to let him spend his money at times so that he could learn to save for a larger item.

"Whoever loves pleasure will become poor. Whoever loves wine and rich food will never be wealthy."

—What is wrong with spending all our money on fun things?

—What should we do with our money?

Further Reading: Proverbs 21:20

DAY 188

Proverbs 21:21 "A person who tries to live right and be loyal finds life, success and honor."

LIVE RIGHT

When Alan was twelve years old, he found himself in a difficult situation. The group of kids he spent time with began participating in activities that he knew did not honor God. The movies they watched, the language they used, their attitude toward the opposite sex, and the type of music they listened to were all things that greatly bothered Alan's conscience. But, these were his friends. What should he do?

Alan felt that God still wanted him to show love to these people, but that he was not to join in their recreation. The result was that years later, these friends came to Alan when their lives ended in shambles. While he had a good marriage and a happy home, many of his friends ended up alone and confused. They wanted what Alan had and he was able to lead them to God who could undo the damage they had done.

"A person who tries to live right and be loyal finds life, success and honor."

—How does living right when we are young bring success and honor to our lives when we are older?

—How can we love others and yet not become like them when they are disobedient to God?

Further Reading: Matthew 5:6; I Corinthians 15:58

DAY 189

Proverbs 21:30 "There is no wisdom, understanding or advice that can succeed against the Lord."

THE LORD ALWAYS SUCCEEDS

When communism came to China, a great persecution began toward many, including Christians. A great many people were imprisoned or killed for their faith. The communist goal was to make sure that they controlled all the practicing religions in their country, which meant that the state was worshiped, not God.

For years it seemed that they were successful, but then in the 1980's when communication was opened freely with the West, we found out that Christianity had not been eradicated. In fact, it had increased. What the communists found out was that they could destroy church buildings and even kill Christians, but they could not remove Christ from people's hearts.

That is the great assurance we have. Nothing can ever take away our relationship with Christ. It is the one thing in the crumbling world that lasts.

"There is no wisdom, understanding or advice that can succeed against the Lord."

—Why can no human system annihilate Christianity?

—What does that mean to us?

Further Reading: Romans 8:36–39

DAY 190

Proverbs 22:1 "Being respected is more important than having great riches. To be well thought of is better than owning silver or gold."

TO BE RESPECTED

Chris and Everett lived on the same street, but that was all they had in common. From his earliest years, Everett had only the goal of being wealthy. He wanted the best house, the best car, and the most expensive clothes.

Chris wanted to make a good living when he was older, but more importantly, he wanted to help others. He became a lawyer in order to take the cases of those who were not rich but were right. He knew he would never be wealthy this way but that he would be serving God through serving others.

Everett made few friends as he sacrificed his family and others to get to the top. He had a lot of things but no one to enjoy them with. Chris made new friends continually as he helped those in need.

"Being respected is more important than having great riches. To be well thought of is better than owning silver or gold."

—Why is being respected more important than being rich?

—How do we become respected?

Further Reading: Proverbs 22:2–4

DAY 191

Proverbs 22:9 "A generous person will be blessed because he shares his food with the poor."

A GENEROUS PERSON

Over a hundred years ago in England, there lived a man named Andrew Murray. Mr. Murray loved God and therefore, loved others. One of his concerns was the great number of orphans in London who had no place to go; no one to care for them, so he began an orphanage.

Andrew Murray was not a wealthy man. Even after giving all he had to the orphanage, there was no way he could provide all the needs of these children. So he began to pray. The miracles God provided were astounding. Unsolicited, the butcher would bring meat, or the baker, bread. Sometimes Mr. Murray would sit down with the children to thank God for the meal before there was any food in the house, yet they never went a day without food.

Andrew Murray knew that "A generous person will be blessed because he shares his food with the poor."

—How are we blessed when we share with others less fortunate than ourselves?

—What do you think God wants you to do to share with others?

Further Reading: Proverbs 19:17

DAY 192

Proverbs 22:21 "I am teaching you true and reliable words. Then you can give true answers to anyone who asks."

TRUE AND RELIABLE WORDS

"Mom, what's wrong with having sex before marriage?" Mandy demanded.

Mandy's mother breathed a quick prayer. It seemed as though every day Mandy challenged something that her mother had taught her. But Mother remained calm and answered Mandy's question.

"Remember what we talked about? God has given you a special gift to give your mate when you marry. Your body is to share with your husband only, no one else."

"But what if you know you are going to marry the person, Mom?"

"You may think you are going to marry the person but you don't know. There is no good reason to disobey God's rules anyway. He knows what is best for us."

Mandy walked away quietly while Mother feared for her. But what Mother didn't know was that Mandy just wanted answers. She took her mother's arguments to school the next day to answer her friends' questions.

"I am teaching you true and reliable words. Then you can give true answers to anyone who asks."

—Why is it so important for parents to teach their children?

—How does this teaching help you to do what is right?

Further Reading: Proverbs 22:17–21

DAY 193

Proverbs 22:24 "Don't make friends with someone who easily gets angry. Don't spend time with someone who has a bad temper."

AVOID A BAD TEMPER

Kurt stormed into the room, throwing his books onto his desk. "Hey Ned, get over here!" he yelled.

Ned looked up. Kurt was his friend but his temper seemed to become worse every day. "What do you want?" Ned answered sharply. He found that he yelled a lot more these days since he was around Kurt.

"Just come here!"

"O.K., O.K., simmer down!" Ned walked to Kurt's desk slowly.

"Do you know what that stupid teacher did last period?"

"Mrs. Allen?"

"Yeah! She gave me a detention! Do you believe that! Well, I'll get her. I'm going to puncture her tires after I leave."

Ned shook his head and walked away.

"Hey, I'm talking to you, Ned!"

But Ned didn't turn around. He knew that Kurt would have to change before they could truly be friends.

—Why should we avoid friendships with people who constantly lose their temper?

—How do such people affect us?

Further Reading: Proverbs 22:24–25

DAY 194

Proverbs 22:29 "Do you see a man skilled in his work? That man will work for kings. He won't work for ordinary people."

SKILL

Nelson loved to make things even as a young boy. As he grew older, he would design furniture that was so beautiful even skilled carpenters took notice. They had to admit that Nelson had an extraordinary talent. But even beyond that, he applied himself. While other kids were watching television, he was perfecting his art. By the time his friends were graduating from college, he had his own business making and designing specialty furniture.

Nelson also used his skill for God. When his church needed a new pulpit, he designed a beautiful one. When an older man in the congregation needed some work done, Nelson volunteered his time and his carpentry skills, giving the man not only a repair job but beauty as well. Nelson knew that he was doing his work for the King of kings.

"Do you see a man skilled in his work? That man will work for kings. He won't work for ordinary people."

—Why is it important for us to work hard in an area we are naturally good at?

—How does God feel if we do not use the talent He has given us?

Further Reading: Matthew 25:29

DAY 195

Proverbs 23:15-16 "My child, if you are wise, then I will be happy. I will be so pleased if you speak what is right."

WISE CHILDREN

Mrs. Vincent and Mrs. Rupert were discussing their children.

"I would love it if my daughter became successful in business. I hope she is rich and comfortable early in life. I don't want her to struggle the way I did," stated Mrs. Vincent.

"I guess I can understand how you feel, but I want something much different for my children," replied Mrs. Rupert. "I think my struggles have made me trust God more and to know Him a lot better. If they become wealthy, that's all right, but most of all I want them to make the right decisions in life."

"I see your point," Mrs. Vincent said thoughtfully. "Maybe I'm looking at my daughter's life all wrong. I just don't know..."

Solomon knew. He said, "My child, if you are wise, then I will be happy. I will be so pleased if you speak what is right."

—Why are the right choices so important to our lives?

—What did Solomon want for his children? Why?

Further Reading: Proverbs 23:22–25

DAY 196

Proverbs 23:17 "Don't envy sinners. But always respect the Lord."

WHO HAS THE BEST LIFE?

"I wish we had a house like Emilie's," sighed Karen. "It has five bedrooms in it and they have three brand new cars. How come we have to be so poor?"

"We're not poor, Karen," her father replied. "We have a nice place to live and although our car isn't new, it runs well. And we've never gone hungry once."

"Oh Daddy! You don't understand. I just want to have one thing better than Emilie's."

"I wouldn't envy her, Karen. Her father has a reputation for being a cold, hard businessman. No one quite trusts him and that would be a sad thing to live with. And besides, they don't know Jesus. That makes us a lot richer than they are!"

Karen couldn't resist a smile. Maybe her dad was right.

"Don't envy sinners. But always respect the Lord."

—Why should we not envy sinners?

—How does seeing how God takes care of us take away our envy?

Further Reading: I Peter 2:1–3

DAY 197

Proverbs 23:29-30 "Some people drink too much wine. They try out all the different kinds of drinks. So they have much trouble. They are sad. They fight. They complain. They have unnecessary bruises. They have bloodshot eyes."

DRUNK

Mr. Cornelius came into the house late just as Elena was going to sleep.

"Where is everybody? Martha come in here," he yelled gruffly for his wife.

"Sit down, Fred," his wife commented firmly as she entered the kitchen. "You are drunk again," she sighed.

"Don't tell me I'm drunk!" he roared. "I'm fine. All of you people have the problem!"

Usually patient, Mrs. Cornelius felt frustrated tonight. "Don't yell at me!" she cried.

"I'll do as I please!"

Elena could hear her father hit her mother as he sometimes did. Then when the reality of what he had done hit him, he began to cry. "I'm sorry, Martha. I didn't mean to do that," he bawled.

Elena didn't believe him. He had said it too many times. One thing she knew. She would never drink alcohol or marry anyone who did.

—What is the problem with being drunk?

—How can alcohol be a trap to those who drink it?

Further Reading: Proverbs 23:31–35

DAY 198

Proverbs 24:1-2 "Don't envy evil people. Don't try to be friends with them. In their minds they plan cruel things. And they always talk about making trouble."

AVOID EVIL

As Mack rode the bus home, he looked sadly at Pete as he sat surrounded by people. Mack would give anything to be as popular as Pete. Everyone thought Pete was funny and smart. He always knew just what to say. Mack decided he would do whatever Pete said if Pete would just pay attention to him.

What Mack didn't know was that Pete was planning to meet some older boys later that evening at the community center. They would introduce him to a man who sold cocaine. Pete also wanted to fit into the crowd. To be accepted by the older boys, he would do whatever was necessary to maintain his popularity. When Pete let himself think about what he was about to do, he felt great guilt about the pain he would cause his mother. So, Pete refused to think about it. His mind was made up.

"Don't envy evil people. Don't try to be friends with them. In their minds they plan cruel things. And they always talk about making trouble."

—Why do we have no reason to envy evil people?

—What will happen to us if we make these people our friends?

Further Reading: Psalm 1

DAY 199

Proverbs 24:3 "It takes wisdom to have a good family. It takes understanding to make it strong."

A GOOD FAMILY

Amy came from a family who regularly attended church and even sent her to a Christian school. Amy heard the truth about God all the time, but she did not grow to love God.

The reason for this was that her parents never spent any time with her. They both worked and volunteered for various groups so they were rarely home in the evenings. They provided well for Amy, but they never talked to her. In fact, her parents never talked to each other. They just lived their lives separately from each other even though they were all under one roof. No one ever spoke to each other in a loving way, or brought questions or problems to each other. As a result, Amy felt that God didn't care about her, either. He just went about minding his own business, but never was interested in what was on her heart.

"It takes wisdom to have a good family. It takes understanding to make it strong."

—How did Amy's family lack wisdom?

—What could they do to make their family strong?

Further Reading: Philippians 2:1–4

DAY 200

Proverbs 24:10 "If you give up when trouble comes, it shows that you have very little strength."

TENACITY

When Anne was eighteen, she decided to go on a summer mission project. The place she went to was just being opened to missionaries, so everything that was done was happening for the first time.

Anne was excited about this mission project because it seemed adventurous and some of her best friends were going along. But when Anne arrived, she found conditions to be difficult. Their beds had not arrived yet from a nearby army base, so she had to sleep on the floor with cockroaches roaming all around her. They had to work long hours during the day, often with little results. After a week of this, Anne was ready to go home.

Fortunately, she had a good friend who challenged her to stay. He reminded her of how much Jesus had done for her. His suffering was much greater than the discomfort she was experiencing. After thoughtfully considering these things, Anne decided to stay. That summer she grew into a committed Christian. She knew she would never live for just her own comfort again.

—Why should we never give up when trouble comes?

—How does "sticking it out" show that we have strength?

—Where do we get such strength?

Further Reading: Proverbs 24:16

DAY 201

Proverbs 24:23b "It is not good to take sides when you are the judge."

BEING FAIR

Matt could hear Owen and John as their argument grew more heated. He decided that it was up to him to try to step in to make peace. As he walked toward them, he thought about what he would say to John. Owen was Matt's best friend. It seemed like John was always picking on him. Matt grew angrier with John by the moment.

"Alright, John, that will be enough. Why can't you mind your own business?"

John looked at Matt with a surprised and hurt expression.

"What have you done now, John?"

"What have I done?" John shouted. "What about Owen? He threw my homework paper into that mud puddle over there. I worked all week on that paper!" John turned and stalked toward his house.

"He must have done something pretty bad to you, huh, Owen?" Matt asked.

Owen hung his head. "I'm afraid not, Matt. I just felt mean and decided to take it out on John. Not too good, was it?"

"I think we both have some apologizing to do. Come on, Owen," replied Matt.

—What was wrong with Matt's attitude when he interrupted the fight?

—What is the best way to judge things rightly?

Further Reading: Matthew 7:1–5

DAY 202

Proverbs 24:26 "An honest answer is as pleasing as a kiss on the lips."

AN HONEST ANSWER

As Mother came through the back door, she heard a crash that sounded like glass shattering. She ran to where the sound had come from and found her two daughters standing over her best china — now just a pile of broken pieces.

Anita looked at her little sister, Paula. "O.K., who wants to tell me about this?" Mother asked, her eyes smoldering with anger and frustration.

"Paula dropped them, Mom. She was carrying them to the dining room table for a tea party," Anita answered quickly.

Paula burst into tears and hugged her mother's leg. "I'm sorry, Mommy. I didn't mean to."

"I know you didn't, Paula. But you know you are not to touch my china. You will have to pay for part of this out of your allowance."

Anita looked at her sister as guilt pulled at her heart. "Mom," she said quietly. "It's my fault. I told her to do it."

Mother hugged her girls and thanked them for their honesty. They still lost some of their allowance but they knew they had done the right thing.

"An honest answer is as pleasing as a kiss on the lips."

—Why is an honest answer so pleasing?

—Why do we need to be honest even if it's difficult?

Further Reading: Psalm 15:1–2

DAY 203

Proverbs 24:27 "First, you should work outside and prepare your fields. After that, you can start having your family."

PREPARE

Kirk and Denise were in love. Although they were only eighteen, they knew they would be in love forever. They decided to get married one weekend. They eloped and told their parents when they returned.

Upon returning home, they realized that they had to find a place to live. However, no one wanted to rent to them since they didn't have jobs. So, they each quickly found jobs as a waitress and a busboy at a nearby restaurant. They were shocked to find out how expensive it was to live. They couldn't afford any of the places they had originally hoped to rent, and they could not pay for any kind of insurance policy. It was tough just saving enough to buy groceries.

Soon Kirk and Denise realized that they should have taken time to prepare themselves financially for their new life together. They would warn their children.

"First, you should work outside and prepare your fields. After that, you can start having your family."

—What should Kirk and Denise have done before they got married?

—What should they do now?

Further Reading: Proverbs 27:23–27

DAY 204

Proverbs 25:9 "If you have an argument with your neighbor, don't tell other people what was said."

KEEP IT TO YOURSELF

Bev was furious. She couldn't believe the things Connie had said to her. The words "stupid and uncoordinated" were still ringing in her ears, the sharpness of them stabbing her like a knife. "How dare she say such things to me! I can't wait to see Courtney. I'm going to tell her how awful Connie is to me."

But before Bev saw Courtney, she heard from her mother. "Did you hear the terrible news about Connie, Dear? She went to the doctor yesterday and found out that she would have to wear a back brace for a year. I guess she is just devastated. Did she seem unhappy today?"

Bev's anger disappeared when she heard what was bothering Connie. She was so glad she hadn't told Courtney.

"If you have an argument with your neighbor, don't tell other people what was said."

—Why should we avoid spreading news about our arguments?

—Who should we tell when we have an argument with another person?

Further Reading: James 3:17–4:1

DAY 205

Proverbs 25:11 "The right word spoken at the right time is as beautiful as gold apples in a silver bowl."

GOLD APPLES IN A SILVER BOWL

Zach walked slowly to school. He was in no hurry to get there. Even though he had really tried to do well in math, it seemed no use. The homework had been confusing to him and he knew it probably wasn't right. Besides that, they were getting a new math teacher today. He dreaded letting her see his poor math paper.

As math period approached, Zach's stomach knotted. When it came time to turn in his math paper, he felt like giving up. Towards the end of the period, the new teacher asked Zach if he could stay a few minutes to talk. Zach wanted to crawl into a hole.

To his surprise, however, the teacher told Zach that the mistake he was making was really a simple one. She told him that with some instruction that he would soon be doing good work. They agreed to work on it together. Zach felt like a new person as he hurried home from school.

—How does the "right word spoken at the right time" do so much for our spirits?

—What can we do to make our words as beautiful as gold apples in a silver bowl?

Further Reading: Proverbs 25:12–13

DAY 206

Proverbs 25:14 "People who brag about gifts they never give are like clouds and wind that give no rain."

THE BRAGGART

Angela had trouble making friends. As a result, she tried to buy everyone's loyalty. Unfortunately, Angela didn't have the money to actually buy the other kids things. So instead she promised everyone lavish gifts. She talked about getting them jewelry and perfume. She spoke of providing free movie tickets and CDs for each of her friends. They soon learned that Angela's promises were empty.

It was too bad, because even those who wanted to be her friend were driven away by her obvious lies. They began to feel they couldn't trust her, so they avoided her.

"People who brag about gifts they never give are like clouds and wind that give no rain."

—What was Angela's problem?

—How did she need to change?

Further Reading: 2 Corinthians 1:12

DAY 207

Proverbs 25:20 "Don't sing songs to someone who is sad. It's like taking off a coat on a cold day or pouring vinegar on soda."

ONE WHO IS SAD

Wayne was hurt inside. His best friend had made fun of him in front of everyone, and then he had walked off with another boy. Wayne had never felt so rejected in his entire life.

Bonnie had seen this happen and she noticed that Wayne looked pretty blue. Thinking she was doing the right thing, she marched over to Wayne and hit him on the back. "Oh, come on, Wayne!" she said. "Don't let them bother you. Let's go in the music room and listen to this new tape I bought. It'll be fun. Come on!" Bonnie then began singing a cheerful song from the tape.

Wayne pulled away from her. "Just leave me alone, Bonnie."

Bonnie left in a huff, mad at Wayne.

"Don't sing songs to someone who is sad. It's like taking off a coat on a cold day or pouring vinegar on soda." She didn't realize that making light of his problem made him feel worse.

—How should we treat someone who is sad?

—What could Bonnie have done to be more sensitive?

Further Reading: John 13:34

DAY 208

Proverbs 25:21-22 "If your enemy is hungry, feed him. If he is thirsty, give him a drink. Doing this will be like pouring burning coals on his head. And the Lord will reward you."

HOW TO TREAT YOUR ENEMIES

Wally was a bully. There was no doubt about it. Every day Pat knew that Wally was going to give him trouble. Wally would always pick a fight with Pat, and Pat would lose his temper with him. The same pattern, day after day, for five years.

One day during family devotions, Pat's dad read Proverbs 25:21, "If your enemy is hungry, feed him. If he is thirsty, give him a drink." Pat began thinking that maybe he could try a different approach with Wally. He would kill him with kindness!

Generally, when he saw Wally, he would go the other way. Today he did just the opposite. Before Wally could get a word out of his mouth, Pat walked over to him. "Hey, Wally, Mom just baked these cookies—want one?" Wally looked at Pat suspiciously but took the cookie. "Do you want to walk to school with me?" For the first time in five years, Wally had nothing to say.

—How are we to treat our enemies?

—Why does this help win them over?

Further Reading: Exodus 23:2–5

DAY 209

Proverbs 25:26 "A good person who gives in to evil is like a muddy spring or a dirty well."

A MUDDY SPRING OR A DIRTY WELL

"Come on, Alex; don't chicken out on me now. You said you wanted to come with me."

"I don't know, Janet; I'm having second thoughts."

"Hey, you said yourself that your folks aren't going to be home after school today. They will never know that you saw this R-rated movie. Don't be a wimp."

Janet finally belittled Alex enough so that she gave in and went to the movie. She had never been to an R-rated movie before. Throughout the movie she felt miserable and uncomfortable. She knew the language, sex, and violence in it was wrong. She thought of her parents and she thought of God. She knew she was letting both of them down. She felt that she was being covered with dirty things.

"A good person who gives in to evil is like a muddy spring or a dirty well."

—Why do we feel so bad when we give into evil?

—How can we avoid "muddying" up our life?

Further Reading: I Corinthians 15:58

DAY 210

Proverbs 25:28 "A person who does not control himself is like a city whose walls have been broken down."

BROKEN WALLS

Charlie had only one goal in life — to have fun. When he was young, this didn't seem to be too bad except that he wanted a lot of new toys. But as Charlie grew, he looked for new, more daring ways to have fun. He tried smoking, alcohol, and even some kinds of drugs. He wasted money as fast as it came to him. He experimented with sex. The trouble with each of these things was that they were fun for a while, but when the newness wore off, Charlie needed more to keep his interest. As a result, Charlie became involved in continually worse things. As a young adult, he already seemed old. His life was in shambles.

"A person who does not control himself is like a city whose walls have been broken down."

—What other interests should have Charlie pursued besides simply having fun?

—Why is a person who does not control himself like a city whose walls have been broken down?

—How can we learn to control ourselves?

Further Reading: 2 Peter 1:5–8

DAY 211

Proverbs 26:8 "Giving honor to a foolish person does no good. It is like tying a stone in a slingshot."

A STONE IN A SLINGSHOT

When the actress walked onto the stage, the audience welcomed her with thundering applause. This was her night. The entire program was given for her honor. She had been an actress for forty years and was admired by many people.

One by one people came forward to tell what an inspiration this actress had been to them. But no one mentioned that his woman had been married many times. She had been a total failure in this area of her life. No one spoke of the way that she neglected her children in order to pursue her own interests. No one mentioned that she had to go against her conscience to play the parts she had taken in many movies.

"Giving honor to a foolish person does no good. It is like tying a stone in a slingshot."

—How was this actress a failure?

—Does the honor she received for her acting excuse her failure in her personal life?

—How does God see this woman?

Further Reading: Proverbs 26:1–12

DAY 212

Proverbs 26:20 "Without wood, a fire will go out. And without gossip, quarreling will stop."

LET THE FIRE GO OUT

"Did you hear about the fight that Jackie and Hannah had?" Joy whispered to the girl next to her. "It was a big one. I doubt they will ever speak to each other again. I guess Jackie slapped Hannah. It almost came to a fistfight!"

Actually, the fight between Jackie and Hannah had not been a big deal, but one girl who witnessed it began spreading the story of it. As it passed along, the story got worse and worse. When it finally got back to Jackie and Hannah, they began to believe that the other was even more at fault. Their anger with each other increased and the fight raged on.

"Without wood, a fire will go out. And without gossip, quarreling will stop." If the gossiping had stopped, the fight would have died out.

—How does gossip make things worse?

—What should be our reaction when we hear gossip?

Further Reading: Proverbs 26:21–28

DAY 213

Proverbs 27:3 "Stone is heavy, and sand is hard to carry. But the complaining of a foolish person causes more trouble than either."

MORE TROUBLE

"I can't believe Mrs. Terrance gave us homework again! What does she think we do all evening? My whole life isn't school!" Calvin fussed as he walked in the door.

"Why don't you just sit down now and get it done, Calvin?" his mother asked.

"I need a break, Mom. I've been sitting and working all day. Those teachers are so mean. They just try to think up ways to make us miserable."

"All I know, Calvin, is that if you spent as much time working as you did complaining, you would be an A+ student. Besides, you complain every day. It gets old after a while, Calvin. Just buckle up and do your work!"

"Stone is heavy, and sand is hard to carry. But the complaining of a foolish person causes more trouble than either."

—What does complaining do to the person who is complaining?

—What does it do to the person who has to listen to the complaining?

—What is the opposite of complaining?

Further Reading: Philippians 4:4

DAY 214

Proverbs 27:17 "Iron can sharpen iron. In the same way, people can help each other."

IRON SHARPENS IRON

When the science teacher stated that humans had descended from animals, Sandy became confused. She had been taught that God made us, but now she wasn't so sure. She thought the teacher was wrong, but how could she know?

The next day in science class, Eric asked if he could speak. He read about the creation in the book of Genesis, chapter one, stating that God made us in his image. He spoke confidently and even the teacher seemed impressed. As Sandy listened, she knew in her heart that what Eric was saying was true. His boldness to stick up for the truth caused her to want to be a more faithful Christian.

"Iron can sharpen iron. In the same way, people can help each other."

—How did Eric help Sandy?

—What are some ways you can help others to be more faithful Christians?

Further Reading: Hebrews 3:13

DAY 215

Proverbs 27:19 "As water shows you your face, so your mind shows you what kind of person you are."

REFLECTION

As Nathan looked into the still pool of water at his reflection, he noticed a lot about himself. His clear, blue eyes and dark brown hair were mirrored in the water, as well as his captivating smile. Nathan knew that when others saw him that they saw someone happy and confident.

But Nathan knew more than his reflection in the pool told. He knew how often he had been disappointed in himself. He had let his friends down, and had hurt his family with his rudeness. He had wished evil on others even as he smiled at them. Everyone thought Nathan was great, but he knew everything that was wrong inside of him.

This knowledge about himself was not bad because it showed him how much he needed Jesus Christ. As he looked at himself in the pool, he prayed that Jesus would turn the bad thoughts into good.

"As water shows you your face, so your mind shows you what kind of person you are."

—How does our mind show us what kind of person we are?

—What can we do with our bad thoughts?

Further Reading: Psalm 7:9

DAY 216

Proverbs 27:20 "People will never stop dying and being destroyed. In the same way, people will never stop wanting more than they have."

WANTING MORE

During one evening of television viewing, I am told that I need a new car to impress my friends, that my husband needs to buy me diamonds to show he loves me, that the right perfume will make me attractive, and that if I wear certain shoes, I will be sought by the NBA.

We live in a very wealthy society that is constantly urging us to buy more. As Christians, we have a responsibility to be different than the rest of the world in this area. We are instructed to think of others as more important than ourselves and to use our wealth unselfishly. We must pay particularly close attention as to whether the purchases we make are fulfilling our genuine need or just adding to our wants. Being a Christian means saying no to our selfish desires.

—Why do we always want more than we have?

—How should Christians be different than the rest of the world in this area?

Further Reading: Luke 18:22–30

DAY 217

Proverbs 28:1 "Evil people run even though no one is chasing them. But good people are as brave as a lion."

RUNNING

Gabe knew he shouldn't have done it. Even now it made him nervous as Mom walked through the kitchen. He had watched her lay down that ten-dollar bill on the counter this morning. It was so easy to slip it into his pocket. Ten dollars was all he needed to pay off the new jacket he had put on lay-away. But now that he had done it, the jacket looked awful to him each time he saw it.

Later that evening, Gabe jumped as his mother called his big brother, Duane, into the kitchen. "All right, Duane," she demanded. "Where's the money?"

"What money, Mom?" Duane asked innocently.

"You know you've been asking me for money all week. Now you just took it. I can't believe it!"

"I would never take your money, Mom," Duane answered in a hurt tone of voice.

Gabe cowered in the living room hoping no one would notice him. He felt terrible.

—What had taking the money done to Gabe?

—Why was Duane brave in his answers to his mother?

Further Reading: I John 2:28–29

DAY 218

Proverbs 28:9 "If you refuse to obey what you have been taught, your prayers will not be heard."

UNANSWERED PRAYERS

Josie couldn't understand why God wasn't answering her prayer. All she wanted was a new dress for the school party. She had been praying for one for weeks now, but obviously God didn't care.

Josie saw God as a big Santa Claus who should give her whatever she wanted. It never occurred to Josie that she wasn't listening to God. She knew that he said in his Word that she should obey her parents, but she didn't want to do that. She knew that she was supposed to love God more than things, but that didn't appeal to her either. She knew the Bible says that we are to love our enemies and help the poor, but why would anyone want to do that!

Josie just didn't get it. Why wouldn't God answer her prayer?

"If you refuse to obey what you have been taught, your prayers will not be heard."

—Why was Josie's prayer not being answered?

—What does Josie need to do?

—Are you obeying the things you know to be true?

Further Reading: John 14:23

DAY 219

Proverbs 28:13 "If you hide your sins, you will not succeed. If you confess and reject them, you will receive mercy."

DO NOT HIDE YOUR SINS

For years, Leon had refused to listen to God. He knew he was supposed to love even his enemy, but he couldn't stand Ned Parker. Ned was a know-it-all who loved to tease Leon. He always made Leon feel as if he were an inch tall, belittling his family, his appearance, and his hobbies.

So, even though Leon knew he was supposed to love Ned, he flatly refused. As a result, every time he saw Ned, his stomach would tie up into knots. Often his whole day was ruined because of Ned's taunts.

After listening to a sermon one day, Leon decided this had to stop. He admitted before God that he was miserable. He asked God to forgive his hatred for Ned and to give him love for him instead. Leon knew it wouldn't be easy, but he also knew Ned would never again ruin his day by making him bitter. Leon was free!

—What happens to us when we hide our sin?

—How do we get rid of sin?

Further Reading: Psalm 32:3–5

DAY 220

Proverbs 28:23 "Those who correct others will later be liked more than those who give false praise."

FALSE PRAISE

Grace had a feeling that what she was about to do was wrong. Her mother had told her not to leave the house while she was gone. But here was her friend, Linda, telling her what a great time the girls were going to have at her house. Surely her mother wouldn't mind so much.

"Come on," Linda urged. "You don't want to miss this. You always do what your mother says. She knows you are a good kid. What's the big deal?"

Just as Linda had Grace convinced, Grace's sister came home. "I wouldn't go if I were you, Grace," her sister reminded her. "Do you remember how long you were grounded the last time you disobeyed her?"

Grace nodded and told Linda she couldn't go. Secretly, she was glad her sister had come home when she did.

"Those who correct others will later be liked more than those who give false praise."

—Why was Grace grateful that her sister came home?

—What was wrong with what Linda told her?

Further Reading: Proverbs 27:5–6

DAY 221

Proverbs 29:6 "An evil person is trapped by his own sin. But a good person can sing and be happy."

DON'T GET CAUGHT IN A TRAP

"I don't care what you say!" Mort yelled at his teacher. "You are just mean to me!"

Every day, Mort was in trouble at school. And everyday he said the same thing, that the teacher was mean to him. In fact, he had said it so many times that he came to believe it, forgetting that his own behavior is what got him into trouble.

As Mort grew older, he treated God just like his teacher. When things didn't go well because of his poor choices, Mort would blame God. If he had only admitted his sin, he would have been able to ask for God's help rather than curse Him. Mort was in a trap.

"An evil person is trapped by his own sin. But a good person can sing and be happy."

—How is an evil person trapped by his own sin?

—How can he escape the trap?

Further Reading: Proverbs 22:5

DAY 222

Proverbs 29:15 "Punishment and correction make a child wise. If he is left to do as he pleases, he will disgrace his mother."

NO DISGRACE

"But Mom, tonight is Maria's slumber party," Mary whined.

"I know, dear, but you knew you had to finish your homework before the party. Since you did not get it done, you must stay home."

"Why can't I do it tomorrow?" Mary cried.

"You will be too tired. Besides, as I said, it was your responsibility to get it done before the party."

"No one else's mother would be so mean!"

"Then no one else's mother cares as much as I do how their child grows up. My love for you causes me to do the hard thing at times."

It was a difficult lesson but Mary needed to understand that, "Punishment and correction make a child wise. If he is left to do as he pleases, he will disgrace his mother."

—How does punishment and correction make a child wise?

—Why shouldn't a child always get what he wants?

—Do adults ever need to be corrected?

Further Reading: Job 5:17

DAY 223

Proverbs 29:18 "Where there is no word from God, people are uncontrolled. But those who obey what they have been taught are happy."

A WORD FROM GOD

John and Rose were neighbors. John's family did not believe in God, so he had never read any of the Bible. The only way John could decide whether something was right or wrong was by trying to figure out what seemed right to him. In some ways, he did all right but in many other ways, his life was a sad confusion. Especially when he became a teenager, John's morality dwindled. He forgot about trying to do the right thing and instead concentrated on doing the fun thing.

Rose came from a family who loved God and instructed her from the Bible daily. When she reached her teens, she was confident that her decisions were the right ones even when everyone around her was doing the wrong thing. Rose had a strong sense of purpose and meaning in her life.

"Where there is no word from God, people are uncontrolled. But those who obey what they have been taught are happy."

—When we ignore God's Word, what happens to us?

—How does obeying God make us happy?

Further Reading: Romans 6:16

DAY 224

Proverbs 29:22 "An angry person causes trouble. A person who easily gets angry sins a lot."

ANGER

As Ruth walked up to her front door, she heard her father yelling again. He spent most of his time yelling anymore. Sometimes he even threw things in his anger. He was mad at Ruth's mother today and she tensed as she heard her mother crying.

About an hour later, Ruth's dad apologized for being angry, but it didn't mean much to Ruth. She knew he would be angry again tomorrow. From reading her Bible, Ruth discovered that her father's anger was sin. Knowing that only Jesus Christ could take away sin, she began to pray that her father would admit his sin to Him and let Him take it away. She knew it was up to her dad.

"An angry person causes trouble. A person who easily gets angry sins a lot."

—How does an angry person cause trouble?

—Why is it sin to repeatedly lose your temper?

—What can we do with our anger?

Further Reading: Proverbs 15:18

DAY 225

Proverbs 30:5 "Every word of God can be trusted. He protects those who come to him for safety."

TRUST HIM

When Adam began to get older, he started to question whether or not the things in the Bible were true. He had doubts from some things he had learned at school and from ways his friends challenged his faith.

One day, he sat down and discussed these questions with his dad. His father answered a lot of them, but it was something else he said that really stuck with Adam.

"Just look at people around you, Adam," his dad had said. "Whose life do you think is better — the one who obeys the things in the Bible or the one who doesn't? Which one has the best family life and is living for things that are worthwhile? Which one would you rather be like when you are old?"

Adam didn't have to think long about it.

—Why can we trust God's word?

—How does His word protect us?

Further Reading: Psalm 12:6

DAY 226

Proverbs 30:7–8 "I ask two things from you, Lord. Don't refuse me before I die. Keep me from lying and being dishonest. And don't make me either rich or poor. Just give me enough food for each day."

JUST ENOUGH

Don had a knack for making money. He was so good at it that it scared him. Don was a Christian and wanted to please God in all that he did. He worried that in making money that he might try to cheat others or cause them hardship. Therefore, Don prayed that God would make him honest. He also prayed that God would help him to be content with just what he needed. He wanted to use his moneymaking ability as a way to give to God. So, he constantly checked himself to make sure he was spending his money on needs and not just wants.

Don memorized Proverbs 30:7-8, "I ask two things from you, Lord. Don't refuse me before I die. Keep me from lying and being dishonest. And don't make me either rich or poor. Just give me enough food for each day." These verses reminded him of what his attitude toward money should be.

—Why did Don memorize Proverbs 30:7–8?

—What are the two things the person in this verse is asking of God?

Further Reading: Hebrews 13:5

DAY 227

Proverbs 30:12 "Some people think they are pure. But they are not really free from evil."

ARE YOU FREE?

Bob went to church every Sunday. He tried to do the right things and most people would say that Bob was a good person. The trouble was that they didn't know Bob's heart. Bob was good to people, but only so they would like him and think that he was a great guy. He went to church, but only because his parents made him. He even read his Bible because he knew that he would be rewarded for it in Sunday school.

So even though on the outside Bob did all the right things, on the inside he was still selfish. Whatever he did, he did to benefit himself. The sad thing was that Bob didn't realize this about himself. He thought he was as good as a person could be — even as good as Jesus Christ.

"Some people think they are pure. But they are not really free from evil."

—Why did Bob think he was pure?

—What evil was Bob not free from?

Further Reading: Luke 18:9–14

DAY 228

Proverbs 31:10-12 "It is hard to find an excellent wife. She is worth more than rubies. Her husband trusts her completely. With her, he has everything he needs. She does him good and not harm for as long as she lives."

AN EXCELLENT WIFE

After Miles and Tom graduated from college, they both began to think about marriage. Tom had always dated girls who were good-looking and ready for fun and laughs. So when it came time to marry, he chose a beautiful girl who loved to party. The trouble was that after they were married, she still loved to party whether Tom was with her or not. His life became a lonely, disappointing thing with his self-centered wife.

Miles was also attracted to beautiful women, but he learned early to get to know a girl's character. As a result, some women who were attractive became ugly to him because of their lifestyle. When he chose a wife, it was a person who was beautiful inside. She was unselfish, giving, and hard working. They had a long, happy marriage. Miles knew he had a great treasure in his wife.

—What makes a good wife? (See verse 12 in Proverbs 31)

—How can a girl learn to be that kind of person before marriage?

Further Reading: Proverbs 31:13–29

DAY 229

Proverbs 31:30 "Charm can fool you, and beauty can trick you. But a woman who respects the Lord should be praised."

CHARM CAN FOOL YOU

Chauncey was the kind of girl who attracted a lot of attention when she walked into a room. Besides looking great, she was outgoing so that everyone noticed her. As people got to know Chauncey better, they became bitterly disappointed with her. Chauncey just used people to make herself happy. No one felt truly loved by her.

Nancy was a quiet girl. People would never pay attention to her in a crowded room, but those who got to know Nancy better grew to love her. She had an unwavering faith in God. As a result, she reached out to all around her, always giving of herself and loving them even when they didn't deserve it.

Chauncey had a lot of friends for a short period of time, but Nancy made friends for a lifetime. In the end, Nancy was the much happier of the two.

"Charm can fool you, and beauty can trick you. But a woman who respects the Lord should be praised."

—How can charm fool you and beauty trick you?

—Why is respect for the Lord so much more important that charm or beauty?

Further Reading: Psalm 112:1–6

ABOUT THE AUTHOR

JoHannah Reardon is the managing editor of Christianity Today's ChristianBibleStudies.com, and she blogs at www.johannahreardon.com. If you enjoyed this book, please give it a positive review. Also, check out her other books:

Children's Fiction: *The Crumbling Brick*
Christian Fiction: *Cherry Cobbler, Redbud Corner, Gathering Bittersweet, Journey to Omwana, Prince Crossing, Crispens Point*

CPSIA information can be obtained
at www.ICGtesting.com
Printed in the USA
BVHW040813170620
581743BV00006B/101